rapid reading naturally:

What it is, How to teach it

By Ben E. Johnson

Quill Publications

117 West Lake Street, Libertyville, Ill., 60048

© Copyright 1976 by Ben E. Johnson
All rights reserved.
Printed in U.S.A.

Published by
Quill Publications
117 West Lake Street
Libertyville, Illinois 60048 U.S.A.

Library of Congress Catalog Card No. 75-44312

ISBN 0-916608-00-X

This book is dedicated to

Bonnie M. Johnson

Friend, Lover, Wife, Mother

and

Reading Teacher,

With thanks for unsaid things.

what is quill publications?

A few years back a need was seen to help authors of merit find a means to bring their ideas to the attention of the public. Some of these authors had developed reputations based on previous writings, lectures and professional expertise, but many were new, young writers never having published, but with fresh ideas. Quill Publications was established to help these writers of merit reach the people that could best benefit from their knowledge and experience. Consequently, we have had enthusiastic support from educators, media people, artists and most important, you the reader. We are concerned that our publications are of high quality and readily available. At present we are attempting to find new works by good writers. These works may be fiction or non-fiction, textbooks or self help materials. It is from you the readers of our present publications that we are hoping to get these future books. We are interested in discussing with writers their ideas as they touch man's relationship to God, to himself, to his fellow man, and to his environment. If you feel you have something to contribute, we would like to hear from you.

acknowledgements

Many thanks are due

Dr. Douglas Frank, Dr. Edward Neteland, Dr. Clark Barshinger, Dr. William E. Nix, Carol Kiehlbauch, and most important, JoAnn McWilliam.

You helped more than you know to make this book and its contents an exciting reality.

TABLE OF CONTENTS

author's preface

Instruction in natural rapid reading (meaning, instruction which uses no machines or programmed materials) has had a tremendous impact on thousands of students in the last few years. Probably the best known and most widely used college level course in natural rapid reading techniques I developed in 1969 and since then has gained acceptance and recommendation from educators and students alike. Participants in this course learned a combination of improved rapid reading and learning skills techniques while practicing on their normal study and pleasure reading. The course was also adaptable enough so that a teacher on another campus could insert his own ideas and study techniques into the basic instruction plan and thus tailor an established course to meet his own students' specific reading needs. This course, called AGP Rapid Reading, has been used by hundreds of schools, colleges, businesses, and churches in the United States and Canada making the AGP course the largest and most successful live-taught rapid reading course today.

In 1969 we conducted experiments to determine the optimum learning time for participants enrolled in rapid reading courses. The objective was to determine the fewest possible hours participants must spend in in-class instruction in order to get the highest increase in reading speed with the best possible comprehension scores. By observing and testing many different groups of people in various length courses, and by feeding all of the data gathered into a computer we determined that the optimum course need only be three weeks long with the students meeting once a week in a two-hour class session. We found that with just these six hours of instruction and with a minimum of 30 minutes a day outside of class spent in reading exercises the average rapid reading student would at least triple his beginning reading and studying speed while at the same time raising his comprehension level. Spending more than three weeks in class sessions was found to be unnecessary. The basic principles of reading improvement could be taught in three weeks. This knowledge was central in the developing of this new comprehension-oriented rapid reading course.

Since then many other "Speed Reading" and rapid reading courses have modeled themselves after the AGP course. The AGP training staff and the author of this book (who is founder and president of AGP, Inc.) have conducted teacher training sessions for hundreds of men and women in the last few years teaching them to successfully conduct a rapid reading course. For the past few years my goal has been to communicate these workable rapid reading techniques as quickly as possible so that the thousands of students presently in our classrooms, workers in business and industry, and laymen in local churches, can have the advantage of knowing efficient reading techniques. This is now possible.

This book discusses the highly successful AGP method of instruction and then step-by-step leads a prospective rapid reading instructor into an understanding of how to set up a good rapid reading course for his school, church or business and with very little expense. With this book and with an interest in helping people read more efficiently, any person can become a rapid reading teacher and can meet some very real reading needs in people.

Ben E Johnson

introduction

the need for rapid reading

the need for rapid reading

The need for an educationally sound course in rapid reading in secondary schools, colleges, businesses, churches and other groups has been obvious for the last decade. School teachers and college professors, parents and employers have recognized the frustration of readers who needed to improve their reading efficiency, but could not afford the cost in terms of both time and money of commercial "speed reading" programs. The cost of the numerous commercially available courses in "speed reading" generally ranged from $75 to $350 and took anywhere up to 15 weeks of in-class time. Add to this the agony of the out-of-class practice required, the daily drills which often took up to two hours a day, and the cost in many ways got to be very high. Also the virtual explosion of information in the last few years has meant that almost everyone has to be able to read and comprehend in a more efficient way than they had been trained to do in the past. Many schools and businesses became concerned that their students and employees weren't being trained in advanced reading the way they felt necessary. What was the answer? Simple: Develop a rapid reading program. But how? No one seemed to know.

The commercially available rapid reading programs attempted to keep what they were doing a secret from nonpaying eyes. Hence, a certain degree of mystery and intrigue has surrounded rapid reading. This also has led to strange excesses in speed reading success claims. It has not been unusual to see advertising claims in the press or to hear them on the radio or T.V. that sound like this: "14 year old girl in New Jersey reads 50,000 words per minute with 90% comprehension. You too can read as fast as you can think." Aside from the fact that these scores are obtained only by mathematical juggling of results, few people ever stopped to think about the impracticality of reading at that rate. In an average book there may be 400 words per page. In order to read at the rate of 50,000 words per minute, the reader will have to turn pages at the rate of 125 pages a minute! The problem here isn't reading fast enough—it's turning pages fast enough! Try some time to turn 125 pages in one minute. There isn't even any time to glance briefly as the pages whiz past. Some programs have even claimed to be able to teach you to read at rates of over 100,000 words per minute while reading backwards.

are machines needed?

Because we are a gadget-conscious nation, many people think that some sort of device is required to improve reading efficiency. Some schools and many courses available to the public advertise the use of gadgets and instruments to solve the problems of the reader—often at a price beyond the reach of a large portion of those who need the help most. Needless to say, the usefulness of these instruments in teaching efficient reading habits is the subject of considerable controversy.

The question is often asked, are machines or other equipment necessary to increase reading rate? The answer, of course, is no. In fact, research tends to indicate that just the opposite may be true. Very often machines are an inhibiting factor to students on the secondary level and above when they are trying to increase their reading rate and efficiency.

Let me cite some research on this subject: Allen Berger[1] declares that research relating to the use of tachistoscopic and pacing devices forces him to conclude that, "At this point in time when teaching groups of students, what can be done with machines can be done as well, if not better, without."

---

1. BERGER, ALLEN. "Are Machines Needed to Increase Reading Rate?" *Educational Technology,* **9 (August 1969), 59–60.**

Robert Karlen[2] reports on 13 separate investigations involving machines and reading instruction done during two decades. These investigations were grouped at four levels—elementary, secondary, college and adult. Karlen found that of the 13 studies measuring instruction in reading where machines weren't used against instruction using machines, 11 of the studies showed that training in natural reading, either equalled or surpassed the machine groups in rate of reading. His conclusion, based on the investigations is that we ought to be spending more money on materials, and less on reading machines.

Many reading instruments can do what they claim to do for the reader, under ideal conditions and with high self motivation of the reader and a determination to persevere through the usually long program. Unfortunately, however, the combination of high cost and a long and involved program whittles away those who actually complete machine oriented reading courses.

Reading devices (most of which attempt to force the eyes to move faster across the line and down the page) can have their place in specialized situations, under the supervision of professionally trained reading instructors, but these devices do involve problems which make their use of questionable value for the vast majority of students. For instance:

1. Transferance of skills from machine to textbook or technical reading is difficult and often impossible. Students only practice in the classroom and on special materials. When the transfer is made to "real life reading" and the machine practice discontinued, reading speed almost always recedes. Therefore, diligent practice using the machines periodically is necessary to maintain gains achieved. The eyes are lazy. They must be constantly forced to keep moving.

2. Also, reading devices generally confine instruction to the individual. It is impossible to set any device to suit a group of participants since individual needs are so divergent. A tachistoscope flashing words on a screen will be flashing faster than the ability of some while below the level of others. Consequently, reading devices are really effectively used only when they are part of individually programmed courses. Most developmental reading labs in schools

2. KARLEN, ROBERT. "Machines and Reading: A Review of Research" *Clearing House,* 32 (1958), 349–352.

cannot accommodate all of the students who require instruction on an individual basis.

3. Professional reading instruments are finely tuned devices, and they are expensive. As reading instruments are introduced into an individual course, the price must rise. The high cost of equipping a reading lab for individual instruction is prohibitive for most schools. Those with well-equipped labs geared for individual programs usually reach only students with most severe problems and consequently don't do the job that is needed among students of average ability.

4. Individual instruction with various reading machines must be spurred by self-motivation. Many, if not most, students do not complete individual programs for lack of desire to keep going. Individual instruction is a lonely road with many casualties.

It would appear, then, that reading devices are valuable when used in a highly controlled setting with selective participants. Their danger lies in considering them as the single answer to the developmental reading needs of *all* students. They are most valuable when used as a complement to group instruction in reading efficiency or as an advanced program beyond classroom instruction.

commercial, school, and college programs

From investigations and surveys of participant attitudes toward rapid reading instruction, we know that participants feel a good rapid reading course (and there are a lot of them) is not a typical speed reading course. To be at its finest it must be inexpensive and as short as possible, placing it within the reach of a great many people who cannot afford the usual higher prices and time involvement of most reading courses. Efficient teaching psychology must be incorporated, making it possible to present the course to large groups without loss of effectiveness. There can be no gimmicks—participants will lose confidence if gimmicks are stuck in. An emphasis in teaching rapid reading courses must be placed on integrating learning skills with improved reading techniques. The stated goal of the course ought to be to develop efficient reading habits and to at least double beginning reading and studying speeds. This goal generally seems practical and attainable to all participants and they know that reading twice as fast will help them immeasurably. The average increase, however, will probably be about three times the beginning rate for nearly everyone, and with at least normal comprehension. Students also feel that rapid reading ought to teach participants not only how to efficiently READ but also how this leads to increased concentration and how increased concentration leads to increased comprehension. What they don't want is a course that claims superspeeds and ignores comprehension. An emphasis should be placed on learning techniques which enable a participant to read different kinds of materials at different speeds.

the need for flexibility

Superspeeds make interesting advertising but they are generally not achievable. *Rapid Reading*—or survival reading—which teaches participants to be flexible readers and to vary their speed for different materials is not only desirable but possible. We all know that there are some things we will always have to slow down on and that there are other things we can speed up on. Unfortunately, most people don't *naturally* know how to fluctuate their speed when they read and besides no one encourages them to vary their speed.

This fluctuation of reading speeds is called "reaming," a word formed from the two words "reading" and "skimming." It is defined as reading with fluctuating speeds varying from slow reading speeds to skimming speeds, even within one paragraph.

For instance, a person may begin reading a paragraph and find that the content is familiar. Without thinking about it, he will increase his reading speed and begin skimming, perhaps passing the words at speeds around 1,200 words per minute. The next sentence read may be technically difficult or unfamiliar, or require complicated reasoning on the part of the reader in order to comprehend what is being said. His speed will drop, perhaps to 150 wpm, and without the reader being aware that he is slowing down to comprehend. The next sentence may again be easily understood or familiar material, and the reader's wpm rate will shoot up to a very high speed again, perhaps 1,000 wpm. This fluctuating speed varying from slow reading to skimming speeds is reaming, or "flexible reading."

a case for group instruction in rapid reading

If reading devices are not the answer to developmental reading instruction, what is? Group instruction. It has been said that the most remarkable reading device in existence is the reader himself. Group instruction such as a good rapid reading course can offer, can use educationally sound principles and techniques of reading improvement, concentrate on group dynamics and simple materials, and can be most effective in developing efficient reading habits. The group dynamics bolster personal motivation, and simple materials and techniques make transfer of learning to technical reading more achievable and more immediately useful. In groups, participants can look around and see that others are trying and succeeding in their efforts. And this may encourage them more than all the teacher's admonitions.

The cost of this kind of group instruction is obviously low since large numbers of people can participate at the same time, expensive devices are not involved, and the length of the course can be shortened by having a simple but achievable goal: to help participants overcome lazy habits, learn basic reading improvement principles applicable to all types of reading, and thereby increase their speed and comprehension.

Just one more thing to remember, a rapid reading course is not a remedial reading course. It cannot solve the reading problems of those who lack basic reading skills taught in elementary schools. These are better left to the trained professional reading specialist. This should be made clear to students, avoiding any false claims of a rapid reading course being a reading cure-all. Rapid reading is intended for the average reader who has developed inefficient habits over the years.

chapter 1
basic concepts in rapid reading

basic concepts in rapid reading

In order for a teacher or a trainer in industry or a staff member in a church to teach a good rapid reading course, it is necessary to understand some basic concepts upon which the entire course ought to be based. These concepts are grouped into three categories: *grouping*, or training the eyes to see more letters with each fixation; *pacing*, forcing the eyes to move at faster or slower rates in different kinds of reading materials; and *comprehension building*, understanding what causes a reader to grasp more of what is being read. If you understand these three major concepts you will understand how any rapid reading course effectively raises speed and comprehension.

reading groups of words

Let's take these subjects one at a time. First grouping. Grouping involves the teaching of the eyes *and the mind* to perceive longer clusters of letters than they are now seeing. Most of us are now taking in 5 to 7 characters every time we stop our eyes, or fixate, on a word or group of words on a page. The following illustrates a poor reader's perception pattern:

Mr. Barbing sat in his rocking chair thinking about
his childhood. It didn't seem possible that the years
had passed so quickly. He could still remember his
high school days when he had squirted the ink from
his inkwell across the classroom with his quill.
College was only a flashing memory. Even the many

A fixation, or a point at which the eyes stop, is represented by each dot, while the arc indicates the span of perception for that point.

We are not physically limited to seeing only 5 to 7 characters, or about one word, every time we stop, but that's how many we do take in. In fact, it's known that we can double that number—we can take in 10, maybe even 15 characters every stop if we have eye training.

To see the span of perception for an efficient reader, note the following paragraph, where the eyes swing farther in each glance:

Mr. Barbing sat in his rocking chair thinking about
his childhood. It didn't seem possible that the years
had passed so quickly. He could still remember his
high school days when he had squirted the ink from
his inkwell across the classroom with his quill.
College was only a flashing memory. Even the many
years he had put in with the firm no longer seemed
significant. Life had passed too quickly.

Reading by phrases is probably one of the best ways to teach students to efficiently understand what they are reading. Bruce Amble[3] summarizes and discusses the implications of three studies relating to phrase reading training for intermediate and junior high school pupils. He concludes that phrase reading training can increase perceptual span, rate, and comprehension for students of all levels of ability. Another researcher, F. B. Robinson[4] declares that college freshmen who were trained in a ten week course to read in spaced phrases of slowly increasing length, increased their speed 28% and their comprehension 5%.

And in a very interesting article, Howard N. Walton[5] discusses the historical background of eye movement studies. Walton points out that at a distance of 16 inches a person can see 1.1 inches on either side of a fixation point. This means he can see relatively clearly three words of five letters each. This also means that it is physically possible for a person to take in approximately three to five words of five letters each with one fixation. However, because we are *physically* capable of perceiving that many words, it doesn't necessarily mean we are *able* to see them.

Now the obvious question is, why aren't we now taking in three to four word phrases when we read? Why are we instead taking in only one word and very often just one syllable at each fixation? To understand this, let's think for a moment about how we were taught to read.

learning to slow down

Remember back in first grade when most of us began learning to read? We were taught to read by reading aloud. We might have been divided up as a class into reading groups, and in each group there was a student picked to read aloud to the rest of the students in that group. The teacher moved from group to group attempting to listen to what was being said as various students read aloud. The other

---

3. AMBLE, BRUCE R. "Reading by Phrases," *California Journal of Educational Research*, 18 (May 1967), 116–124.
4. ROBINSON, F. B. "An Aid for Improving Rate," *Journal of Educational Research*, 27 (February 1934), 453–455.
5. WALTON, HOWARD N. "Vision and Rapid Reading," *American Journal of Optometry*, 34 (1957), 73–82.

students listened to what was being read. But what happened every time a student came to a new word that he didn't know? Well, it might happen something like this. The student might be reading, "See—Dick—and—Jane—go—to—the—parapsychologist." Well, it's not likely that such a word would appear, but if such a word did appear, the student reading would come to the word "parapsychologist" and would probably start saying "Pa . . . Pa . . . Pa . .", and stuttering, trying to pronounce the unfamiliar word. At that point the teacher usually interrupted and said, "Slow down and sound it out."

And so the student, and all of us for that matter, got in the habit of slowing down and sounding out each new word, syllable by syllable. And nearly every word was a new or unfamiliar word in those early years. Now this continued, breaking up the words we were learning into as small units as possible, usually syllables, for years and years. Thus we built into ourselves the tendency, every time we came to a new word or an unfamiliar word, to break it up into small units.

When were we instructed in putting those words back together again? When were we given any grouping training? Seldom were any of us fortunate enough to have that kind of training. Because of this we built into ourselves the habit of looking for the smallest possible units each time our eyes stopped to fixate when we read. Well, what do we do about this? Obviously, we've got to do something to increase our span of perception if we're going to increase our reading efficiency.

reading by phrases

We learn again and again that the single greatest problem in teaching students to group words is not in convincing them that they *can* see longer groups of letters at one glance, because most people believe that that is quite possible. The problem is *how* to teach students to see clusters of letters at increased spans and speeds of perception when they are not being forced to do so by some mechanical device. With these problems in mind, phrase reading training exercises have been developed which are designed to increase the span and speed of perception, while at the same time transferring this grouping ability to real-life reading. What are these exercises?

These grouping exercises are spelled out for you in more detail later in the book under the rapid reading instruction section, but let me summarize them here for you: First, each week rapid reading course participants are asked to do approximately ten minutes a day of grouping exercises. The first week they are asked to take a single page of print and to divide each line into circled phrases.

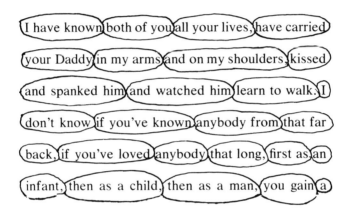

I have known both of you all your lives, have carried your Daddy in my arms and on my shoulders, kissed and spanked him and watched him learn to walk. I don't know if you've known anybody from that far back, if you've loved anybody that long, first as an infant, then as a child, then as a man, you gain a

After they have divided each line into circled phrases, they must read that page of circles every day for ten minutes. They should go back and forth over the circled phrases looking not at the words in the circles, but instead looking at the top of each circle as fast as they can. To help this along they should use their index finger to point at each cluster of words. This causes them to move very rapidly across and down the page hopping their eyes from phrase to phrase. This begins to accustom them to seeing *clusters of words* rather than a few letters. Participants should do this every day for ten minutes a day for the first week. By the end of the week they will have become so familiar with that page that they will begin to see groups of words without even thinking about the target that surrounds each word. In fact, what they begin to do is to turn the circled page occasionally and to start seeing the uncircled words on the next page as if they were circled.

We learn from studies in educational psychology that the mind tends to think in patterns and since for a week students have been looking at that same page of print, reading it over and over again, seeing circles about it, when they turn to pages of print that are not circled, they have established a pattern and have begun to develop a tendency to see circles around those words also. Thus, *they begin to think in terms of groups.* For ten minutes a day for one week students are asked to do this. Actually, it's psychological conditioning rather than physical conditioning. By the end of the week students are beginning to look for natural units of words rather than to simply look at each word and the syllables in it.

slashing

Starting the second week participants are asked to do a similar drill for ten minutes a day and an important weaning process begins which eventually will enable the class members to group words without aid of circles or gadgets. This second week they are asked to take another page of print and again to use that same page every day for ten minutes. But instead of circling, this time they put *slash marks* at the beginning and end of the phrases in each line.

jutting edge / of the rocky precipice / echoed in my mind

/ as I stood / alone on the opposing / shore / remembering

/ the love / I had lost. Reflecting upon / the moments of

joy / I had shared / in the past, my cold / and shivering

body / became intoxicated / with the warmth of memory. /

Even if / there was a storm, / I could see / the calm rising

/ of a restful dawn.

Thus participants begin eliminating the target circle around the words leaving just beginning and end marks to remind them that they are looking for groups. They are to go over and over this same page of print, getting used to seeing clusters without circles.

Beginning then the third week participants are given what is called the grouper card.

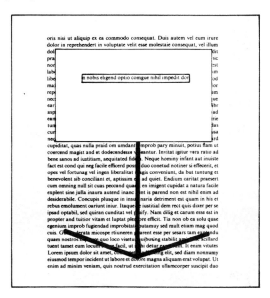

This is simply a 3 × 5 card that has a center rectangle to be cut out. This little slot will expose a cluster of words on the page of print. Participants are asked to place the card on a page of print and to pull the card straight down the page from line to line, exposing a small group of words on each line. As students pull the card from line to line, normally what they will see in the slot is the tail-end of one word, maybe the whole second word and the beginning of a third word. After practicing with this grouper card for a few days students will find that they are able to pull the card from line to line with increasing speed because their span of perception has gotten accustomed to that width of phrase. When this happens they simply widen the slot. When they widen the slot they widen their perceptual span and must start all over again pulling the slotted card from line to line trying to make sure they see everything that is in it, while still moving as rapidly as possible from line to line.

Gradually over a period of two or three weeks class members will find that they have usually widened their span of perception to twice their normal span of perception. When that happens, participants turn the card over and cut out the two slots at the bottom of the card. They then slide the two-hole grouper down the page, glancing quickly at each slot.

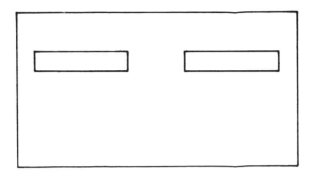

This complicates their reading just a little bit. They have to quickly hop their eyes to take in two clusters of words per line, thus helping them develop a rhythmic eye swing.

As class members hop their eyes back and forth across a line trying to see as fast as they can the words that are in the slots, they will find that they become accustomed to the slot sizes and they can perceive words in two slots almost as quickly as they could see words in one slot. When this happens they should widen the slots toward the middle. As they continue to widen the slots toward the middle, gradually the center obstacle of the card between the slots is diminished, until finally there comes a point when the center obstacle can be completely eliminated. At that point students are simply looking at one line of print, hopping their eyes back and forth at rapid speeds. And they have been weaned from needing any grouping device. They can throw away the grouper card and simply hop their eyes back and forth on lines of print because they have accustomed their eyes to taking in clusters of words at normal speeds of perception. More about this later.

pacing

Now, let's take up another major concept in a good rapid reading course. The concept of pacing.

A matter that needs clarification at the outset is that we read different materials at different speeds. A novel can be read much faster and much easier by most people than can a logic or philosophy book because the ideas in the logic or philosophy book are much harder to understand and must be read slower to comprehend the concepts. But something else that must be very clear is that we can increase reading speed in *both* the easy reading *and* the difficult reading. If they double their speeds in light reading by following the principles set up for them, they can also double in heavy reading by following the same principles. Now these speeds may be considerably different: for instance a student may double in light reading from 250 to 500 WPM but by using the same reading principles he should also be able to double in that philosophy or logic book, say from 100 WPM to maybe 200 WPM. The principles of rapid reading may be applied to all types of reading and should enable participants to pace themselves at various speeds with various kinds of material.

But what exactly is pacing? Pacing is defined as forcing the eyes to move in directed patterns across the line and down the page. Now, did you notice the four parts of the definition? Pacing is defined as, first, *forcing*. The eyes won't move by themselves. You can't simply say to your eyes, "Eyes, read faster" and expect them to do it. They won't—they somehow must be forced to move. Second, they must be *directed*. The eyes have to be taught which way to move and how to move. For efficient reading they must have direction and pattern to follow, rather than randomly moving down a page. Third, *across the line*. As long as words are written across the line, that's the way our eyes will have to move. We cannot zip down the middle of a column or down the middle of a page and expect good comprehension. We must follow across the line. Fourth, *down the page*. The eyes must be trained to move efficiently from line to line.

How does pacing fit into rapid reading training? Basically, there are two major problems to overcome when it comes to learning rapid reading. The first one, the problem of fixation, we covered already when we discussed the subject of grouping. We stop too often because we can't take in enough letters at one glance, and we stop too long on each fixation.

regression

The second major problem in reading is the problem of regression. Regression is the eyes' tendency to flick back over what has been previously read in an attempt to reassure the eyes that what they really saw, they really saw. This is normally a subconscious desire on the part of the reader to check up on himself. This occurs especially with long words or unfamiliar words or concepts. We've all had the experience of reading along a line and all of a sudden finding ourselves back on a word that we've just read before.

It is difficult to avoid the conclusion that smaller

schools will find it necessary to rethink their roles as

the task of providing funds for adequate operation

becomes more formidable. Already there is a grow-

ing conviction that modern education must lay aside

the once hallowed idea of the value of small institu-

tions and accept the notion that quality professional

education demands a sizable heterogeneous com-

Now, actually we are not conscious of our eyes jumping back to look at a word a second time. All we know is that we are there, we're back. Because the eyes move so rapidly we can't tell when they flick back. Only sophisticated eye cameras, ophthalmographs, can measure how fast the eyes move back and forth across the line. But we are conscious that we're suddenly back on a word that we've already read, and that's called regression. It is an unconscious movement of the eyes back along the line when we ought to be going towards the right hand side of the page.

Now, how serious a problem is regression? Quite serious. For some inefficient readers, regression may occur anywhere from 50% to 60% of the time. This means that for every ten words the eyes move forward, the eyes may flick back in regression five or six times. These readers will take a relatively long time to get across a line of print. Again let me remind you that we're not conscious of our eyes flicking back all the time, but we do know that regression takes place. In an average reader, regression may take place 40% of the time. Obviously this is a hindrance to high speed and improved comprehension.

There are many kinds of regression. For instance, there is the kind of regression where you read along the line and all of a sudden find your eyes pulled up to a word or phrase on the next line. In another form of regression you read along the line and then begin to make a return sweep back to the beginning of the next line and all of a sudden you find yourself three lines too far down or perhaps two lines too far up. What happened? Was it an accident that you missed the line that you were supposed to be on and started reading on the wrong line? No! Your eyes were pulled off target by some other word. In fact, think of the millions, literally millions of times when you have been reading along a line and you came back and hit the beginning of the next line as you had planned to do. What happened this time? Return sweep regression occurred and pulled you off target. Your eyes were not following directed patterns, they were simply being attracted in other directions by other words. Well, if regression is this kind of problem, what can we do about it? We can learn to pace ourselves when we read.

direct the eyes

We can push the eyes across the line and down the page in a regular rhythm, thus keeping the eyes from flicking back. Reading machinery uses a variety of levers, bars and shadows to keep the eyes moving ahead, but they have problems. An alternative is suggested by pacing. There is a growing popularity for what is called the hand pacing method, or natural reading method, of rapid reading. This approach uses the movement of the hand to force the eyes to move across the line and down the page. It does the same thing as a reading machine but is much more versatile. Using the hand as a pacing device, participants can practice on all kinds of materials, both in class and out of class. It's the kind of exercise they can practice wherever they are, whether they are riding in a bus, a plane or simply sitting in the classroom. The flexibility is obvious, but what is even more obvious is the lack of any cost. Every student comes equipped with his own pacer. Let me explain.

If you take a book, right now, and time yourself to read for three minutes at your normal reading rate, you will probably come up with a reading rate of 250 to 350 WPM. On the other hand if you take that same book, making your index finger serve as the pointer and begin reading while sliding your fingertip under the line and slightly ahead of where you are reading, you will find that you read much faster because your eyes will follow the motion of the pacing finger, eliminating much regression. If you will read using your finger as a pacer, pointing at the words that you're reading, sliding it ahead of your eyes, you will find that this pacing pulls your eyes across the line and from line to line at a much faster rate than ever before.

You will also find that when pacing you will have a tendency to eliminate unnecessarily long fixations on words because keeping your finger moving from line to line develops a rhythmic movement which doesn't permit you to stop unnecessarily long on any one word.

But another thing you will find when you use your hand as a pacer, pointing at what you are reading, sliding your hand faster and faster along the line, is that you will develop increased powers of comprehension. In fact, you will find that you develop strong eye-hand coordination. This simply means that you become both physically and mentally involved in reading. This causes your concentration to be much more intense. That probably never happened before. Most people simply pick up a book and start to read. Now, however, using your hand as a pacer, forcing your eyes along the line, you will find that you are concentrating much more than ever before. As a result you have higher levels of comprehension. The more you concentrate on what you're reading the more your comprehension is going to go up. Think of it this way—we can call it eye-hand coordination, but another way of describing it is to say that if you pace yourself with your hand you will probably never again fall asleep while reading!

basic z

When you begin pacing yourself across the page by using your hand as a pointer, you will begin doing what is called the Basic Z pacing pattern. It is called the Basic Z because it looks like a Z. Using your pacing finger you pull your eyes across the line and back to the beginning of the next line in rapid fashion. The design of your finger on the page traces something that looks like a Z pattern. This emphasizes the across the line pull for the eyes.

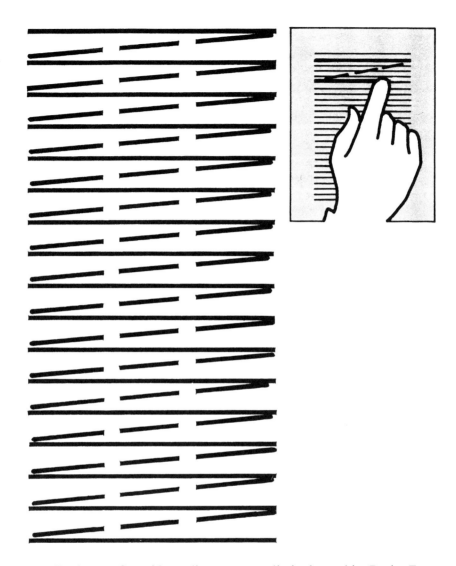

Students of rapid reading are not limited to this Basic Z movement. In fact, in a rapid reading course, we suggest several different pacing movements and ask participants to try to pace themselves once or twice with each pattern in an attempt to find a way of reading and pacing which is both efficient and comfortable. You will find that your participants immediately will catch on to pacing as they read.

In a rapid reading course you should teach your class members to pace themselves so that they will be independent of reading machines or any other mechanical reading device. Now, the question always arises, will rapid readers always need to pace themselves every line, word by word, as they are reading? Well, that question can be answered with a yes and a no. Yes, class members will always need to force themselves to keep reading faster because when they stop pacing they will quickly fall back into the old habits of reading and they will slow down. But no, they will not always need to pace themselves the same way that they first paced themselves. Many will find that after practicing for awhile they need only to pace themselves every third or fourth line in order to keep their speed up, or every second or third page.

Class members ought to be encouraged to sophisticate the concept of pacing for themselves. But with all of this we suggest that participants concentrate not so much on the specific motion but instead concentrate on the idea of movement on a page and what it does. It is the movement on each line or on each page which causes us to overcome most regression and fixation problems and encourages us to be much more attentive to the materials we are reading. Knowing this, students of rapid reading very quickly can develop their own methods of pacing themselves.

comprehension building

Now, let's discuss the third major emphasis necessary in a rapid reading course: comprehension building. One of the things that we are well aware of in rapid reading is that the kind of reading students of rapid reading are concerned with is survival reading. They are not reading because they *want* to read most of the time, but they are reading because they *have* to read and therefore they must learn as they read. Thus, they cannot speed through the pages at some fantastic superspeed level and skim everything. They must concentrate on what they are reading and they must comprehend it. But how do we help participants to raise their comprehension? Essentially, there are three ways to build comprehension.

expect better comprehension

First, students ought to expect better comprehension. Now that sounds rather simple, but let me give you an illustration. There was an experiment conducted some time ago with two sixth grade classes. The two classes were given the same kind of instructions, curriculum, and as much as possible the same kind of classroom teaching. In fact, everything was kept as much alike as possible for one entire school year. There was, however, one difference—the difference was that at a certain time each day both sixth grade classrooms were given a reading assignment. In one class the students were told to read specific pages and that was all. The other sixth grade class, at exactly the same time was given the same reading assignment, but they were also told in a few words to read for comprehension. "Know what's there. Make sure you understand what you're reading." Every day for the entire school year they were given this admonition. They weren't told that they were going to be tested. They were simply told to stress comprehension. At the end of that year, both classes went through a series of tests and what do you think the difference in scores was? You probably guessed correctly—in the second class where the students were told every day to expect good comprehension, the comprehension level was 60% higher than the other sixth grade class where they were not emphasizing content.

Now, why did this increase come about? The teacher hadn't said anything about giving a test, but the students had guessed from the constant emphasis on comprehension that they were probably going to be held accountable for what they were reading at some time in the future. They also got the impression from the teacher that knowing content was very important. And thus they were hard on themselves—they were reading for comprehension rather than just reading.

Now that's the point we need to get across to our class members—that they must read for comprehension and that they can be the single greatest check on whether or not they are getting it. They must expect better comprehension, and adjust their speeds so that they always read for information, otherwise they won't get good comprehension.

read with a questioning mind

There is a second way to build comprehension. It can be called the active vs. the passive approach. That simply means that students who read with an active and questioning mind will always have a better understanding of what they read than those with a passive approach to reading. Again, an illustration: When I first started teaching some years ago, I taught courses in English and Literature, and one of my favorite courses was an upper level course in the poetry of the Romantic period: Wordsworth, Coleridge, Byron, Keats, Shelley. For every class period I would give my students a reading assignment that might sound like this: "Read pages 40 through 60 for next class period—class dismissed." Then, because I wanted to encourage them to keep up with the reading assignment, each day when they came back to class I would give them a quiz based on that class period's assignment. And do you know what I found out? I found out that those students just didn't seem to have the answers. They seemed to be losing comprehension rather than gaining it as we went on through the semester.

I decided after a short period of time to change the way I gave the assignments. I started saying, "The reading assignment for next class is pages 40 through 60, but in those pages I want you to find five themes that seem to come up all the time. I want you to find six subjects that Wordsworth and Coleridge have in common. I want you to find seven images that are used consistently in Wordsworth's poetry." And questions like that. When the students came back to class after that and I gave them a quiz, it was amazing—the students now had much better comprehension. Why? What made the difference?

The difference was that they were now reading actively rather than passively. They were reading with a questioning mind, they were looking for answers, they were reading with a purpose and the purpose was no longer just to get from page 40 to page 60 as it had been in the past. The purpose was now to find some information.

An interesting study was done by a man named Ebbinghaus in 1885 and has been done often since then and with the same results. It charts how quickly we forget. This study shows that the average person, when handed a book and told to read it, and then questioned on it, within 20 minutes will loose 42% of the information. As he gets farther and farther away from the moment of reading, he will lose increasingly more and more information until within a week to 10 days he will have forgotten 90% of everything he read. But, the results are no longer the same when you hand a person that book and you say to him, "Look, raise some questions over what you are going to read before you read it. Speculate on it for a few moments. What do you want to know about this book?" This forces him to start reading with a questioning mind. After he reads the book and you start questioning him, the difference in retention is amazing. The same person reading now with a questioning mind who earlier forgot nearly everything within just the first few days now will get twice the comprehension, and he will retain it for a much longer period of time.

Now what made the difference? The difference is the questioning mind. If we make ourselves conscious of what we want to know, if we know the questions that we would like answered as we begin reading, if we question before we begin reading, our eyes and perceptions will have a tendency to seek out and note the answers when we come anywhere near them. In essence we are reading for answers to questions and we have heightened our perception and concentration.

previewing and postviewing

A third way to build comprehension is to instruct participants in the method of previewing and postviewing. This is one of the best ways for people to immediately see how comprehension is built. The average number of pages for each reading assignment for most students in college is 35. Think with me for just a moment—what if when a student picked up a reading assignment and began to read those 35 pages, he first forced himself to glance at every single page very rapidly before he began reading? What if he covered those 35 pages in five minutes? What would he remember? He would remember having seen factual things, proper nouns, names, dates, captions, italicized words, that kind of thing. He would find he had given himself an overview of what's in the assignment. You can see what this would do. This would enable him to form some questions over what he was about to read. He could speculate on what's in the reading. He could anticipate what's coming so that it would seem quite familiar when he began reading it.

What is going to be the effect of this previewing on his reading? Since the reading will now seem a little bit familiar, he is going to have a tendency to read it faster, and he's going to have a tendency to find the answers to the questions that he has been raising. His comprehension is going to go up and he is reading much faster.

But what happened at the end of the assignment? He completed the reading, is he finished? No. What he needs to do now is postview. What is postviewing? Postviewing is simply taking another five minutes and again moving very rapidly, glancing at every page, and re-reading the entire 35 pages in five minutes. What do you think the reader sees now in this quick rush through the pages? You might be surprised at the answer. He doesn't necessarily see the things that the author considered important. In fact, the reader has no control over what he sees. His eyes have a tendency to seek out and to read again those things that struck him as being important, unusual or interesting when he was reading. It's a reinforcing effect, and it's great for retention. A person who will take a few moments to preview anything he reads before he reads it and who will postview after reading it, will find that his comprehension goes up dramatically. How much extra time has he spent doing this? Maybe an additional ten minutes, but what did he get out of it? What he received is an increased reading rate. He's reading much faster and at a dramatically increased comprehension level.

in summary

How do we build comprehension?—*three ways*; First we must ask our students to become conscious of their comprehension, to expect better comprehension. Second, we try to get them reading actively rather than passively. Reading with a questioning mind—reading with a purpose, attempting to determine what they want out of the reading material, and then finding it as they are reading. And third, we encourage students to always preview and postview.

chapter 2
things to get ready

things to get ready

the instructor and his aids

The most important single factor in a successful rapid reading course is not the materials, the students, or even the program; it is the instructor. He will be a *guide* and *encourager*. The latter is at least as important as the former. The confidence which the participant has in himself will influence the rapidity and success with which he learns the skills of rapid reading. To foster this self-confidence, you should work to construct a positive classroom spirit and healthy group dynamics. Your own buoyant, optimistic manner will be of great help, as will your sense of involvement with the participants, your encouraging spirit and your approval of their successes.

Try to build the mood among your participants that the rapid reading course is a gigantic group experiment. Encourage the feeling that you are all together to try some new things which could prove exciting; to this end, strongly urge all class members to try each *technique* and each drill just as you describe it, at least once. Later, if a technique proves uncomfortable or ineffective they can—and will—ignore it, but they should all give it at least one chance.

You will want to get as much feedback as possible on almost every aspect of the course. Ask questions of the class frequently, especially to learn the most recent words-per-minute rates achieved, and it might not be a bad idea to have hands raised occasionally so that the whole class can see the good progress of their fellows. For example: "How many of you have now already doubled your beginning rates?" "Is there anyone here who has passed the 800 wpm mark yet?" It will encourage the less successful participants to keep trying if they see classmates having good success. Also ask questions concerning the obstacles that the students are facing. You will want to keep reminding participants to read for normal comprehension. This way the class members will see that they are not alone in their struggles.

The suggestions outlined in this book will work if you apply them in the manner outlined. However, you will discover that the presentation is lifeless and less effective if you do not inject your own personality and ideas into it. Use your materials as the spirit of the class dictates. Above all, a good sense of humor will do wonders for the class spirit. After all, what we basically are doing is altering a human behavior pattern that each one has had for 10, 20 or more years. To alter this is a bit difficult for some people, and they are nervous or worried, and in need of assurance. Your easy going, non-selling "try it" attitude will go a long way toward easing tensions and setting a good learning atmosphere.

The Stopwatch

A stopwatch is necessary to the smooth operation of a reading session. The watch need not be an expensive model, just one with which you can accurately time the reading drills. Reliance on a wall clock in the room is not recommended as it is not nearly as flexible and responsive as the stopwatch. The psychological effect of an official timing device will also be of benefit to the attitude and performance of your students.

Weekly Summary Cards

To assist your instruction we recommend that you use weekly summary cards of what you wish to say. These three cards provide the instructor with a brief cue for pacing the instruction each week. Each step of instruction is correlated on the weekly summary card to the class session section in this book and to the transparency numbers. You will want to keep the appropriate card handy during your class sessions to serve as a quick reminder of what comes next in the course. Samples are included here.

SESSION 1 — INSTRUCTOR'S SUMMARY CARD — 1st Hour

OBJECTIVE	EVENTS	TRANS. #	SUGGESTED TIME
Learner finds out where he is.	1. Objectives–Why are you here?	1	5 minutes
	2. Registration Card–Motivators	2 3 4	25 minutes
	3. Reading Tests–Novel and Minnesota (Form A)		
	4. Three Types of Reading Material	5	
Learner finds out what causes this and what to do about it.	5. Problems in Reading	6 7	30 minutes
	6. Regression/Fixation; Pacing Introduction	8 9	
	7. Eyes Follow Motion–Basic Z	10 11	
Learner tries and gets feedback.	8. Timed Test (enter on card or use Event #12 for card)		
	9. Break		5 minutes

SESSION 1 — INSTRUCTOR'S SUMMARY CARD — 2nd Hour

OBJECTIVE	EVENTS	TRANS. #	SUGGESTED TIME
	10. What About Details?	12	10 minutes
Learner tries again, with feedback	11. Rapid Reading Rules	13	10 minutes
Learner finds a second cause and what to do about it	12. Acceleration Helps; Timed Test	14	10 minutes
Learner tries it with feedback	13. Grouping Instruction (Refer to Problems)	15	10 minutes
	14. Grouping Drill I (Circling Phrases)	16 17	10 minutes
	15. Pacing Movements Summary; Wiggle		
Reinforces prior learning	16. Pacing Drill I (Fast, Fast, Fast)	18	5 minutes
	17. Timed Test to put together new skills, Enter on card, note comprehension.	12	
	18. Summary	19	
Motivate learner to use to gain personal benefits	19. Assignment–Motivate to Use New Skills	20	10 minutes
	20. A. Collect registration cards B. Leave books C. 10 minutes grouping. 20 minutes pacing is minimum use.		
			2.0 hours

32

SESSION 2
INSTRUCTOR'S SUMMARY CARD
1st Hour

OBJECTIVE	EVENTS	TRANS. #	SUGGESTED TIME
Overview	1. Welcome & Review	19 21	10 minutes
Learner finds out where he is.	2. Timed Test (enter results)		5 minutes
	3. Fixation Card		10 minutes
	4. Reteach Grouping	22	10 minutes
Learner sees what to do about it and tries it.	5. Grouping Drill II (Slashing)	23	5 minutes
	6. Pacing: Hop– Fit to Grouping	24	5 minutes
Learner sees another benefit and tries it.	7. Comprehension Bldg. I. Questioning Mind II. Previewing	25 26	15 minutes
	8. Timed Test (enter on card)	25	5 minutes
	9. Break		5 minutes

SESSION 2
2nd Hour

OBJECTIVE	EVENTS	TRANS. #	SUGGESTED TIME
Learner finds out where he is.	10. Vocalizing (optional)	27	5 minutes
	11. Pacing Drill II (3X3)	28	15 minutes
Learner breaks old habits by trying it. with feedback.	12. Pacing–Arrow	29	
	13. Preview Exercise	30	15 minutes
	14. Comprehension Bldg.		
Learner tries a comfort pattern	15. Pacing–Curve	31	5 minutes
Learner re-learns fuzzy or weak points	16. Review Pacing and Grouping		5 minutes
Learner puts it all together	17. Timed Test (enter on card; note comprehension)	16	5 minutes
	18. Review, answer questions	21	5 minutes
	A. Collect cards B. Leave books C. Minimum use is 30 minutes a day, but challenge them to read a book a week.		
			2.0 hours

33

SESSION 3 — INSTRUCTOR'S SUMMARY CARD — 1st Hour

OBJECTIVE	EVENTS	TRANS. #	SUGGESTED TIME
Find out where the class is.	1. Welcome & Review	19 21 32	10 minutes
	2. Timed Test (enter results)	12 16	5 minutes
Learner sees benefits of changing behavior	3. Grouping Drill III (Grouper Card)	33	10 minutes
	4. Pacing: Comfort Motions— Crosshatch. Zigzag	34 35	5 minutes
	5. Pacing Drill III (Many Fast/Few Slow)	16 36	10 minutes
Learner sees the difference between Skimming and Scanning	6. Skimming and Scanning	37	15 minutes
	7. Timed Test		5 minutes
	8. Break		5 minutes

SESSION 3 — 2nd Hour

OBJECTIVE	EVENTS	TRANS. #	SUGGESTED TIME
	9. Learning & Study Skills		5 minutes
	10. Pacing Comfort Patterns— Loop. Spiral	38 39	10 minutes
Learner tries new skills which may benefit him— with feedback time.	11. Comprehension Bldg. III A. Notetaking; read and note in books. B. Postviewing	40 10	5 minutes
Learner finds out where he is *now* compared to start.	12. Final Tests A. Novel–Note comprehension B. Minnesota or Bendic. Form B.		15 minutes
	13. Enter comments on back of registration card		5 minutes
	14. Review and Conclude: A. Collect cards B. Leave books C. Minimum use is 30 minutes a day for 6 more days; 10 min. grouping 20 min. pacing D. The Course is Not Over!	19 21 32 41	10 minutes
			2.0 hours

The Transparencies

Visual aids are in large part responsible for the effectiveness of the transfer of learning in a good rapid reading course. You should become thoroughly acquainted with the overhead projector transparencies which parallel and compliment the instruction, and master their use so that your teaching with them becomes a very natural and smooth process. Copies of the transparencies used in teaching the AGP Rapid Reading course are included in an appendix at the end of this book.

Some transparencies are used each session, others only once, although you will alter their use to fit your needs. The transparencies ought to be numbered for quick reference and for aid in determining sequence. There are several categories, not directly related to numbering, into which the transparencies fall:

a. used each session
b. introduction and review
c. concluding and motivating
d. facts and data
e. pacing
f. grouping
g. study skills

You may want to write your own notes on the transparency frames to keep important points and your own interjections in mind as you use them.

materials and physical arrangements

The Room

Although room conditions vary, there are certain requirements for effective learning. The room should be well lighted and the temperature controlled for comfort. Since the rapid reading course is often taught in the evening, after many of the participants have had a busy day, a room that is too warm or dimly lit will induce drowsiness and reduce concentration.

Set out books for practice reading at the rear of the room if possible. Let your students make their own choice of books. These should be set out well in advance of class time so that participants can peruse the selection as they arrive and take their time in choosing the books that interest them. Make suggestions but never pick a book for anyone. If you assign the books the participant often feels relieved of responsibility for results since "teacher assigned this one to me and I don't like it."

In the inside front cover of each book make certain that the average number of words per line and the average number of words per page for that book has been indicated. This will assist participants in computing their word per minute (wpm) rate on various timed tests during the course.

Room size is dictated by the number of participants enrolled. Technically there is no limit to the number that may be taught in one class. Experience will teach you how many you can effectively and comfortably teach and with what size classes the group dynamics are best. The ideal is probably around 25, but AGP teachers have effectively conducted classes with as many as 350 participants. Since it is not necessary to work with each student individually, you are only limited by the number who can easily view the overhead projector and see and hear you.

Overhead Projector

An overhead projector is necessary in teaching an efficient course. The overhead projector and screen must be at the front of the room. Place the projector or rearrange the desks so that every participant can see the screen. The following diagrams illustrate good projector/screen position.

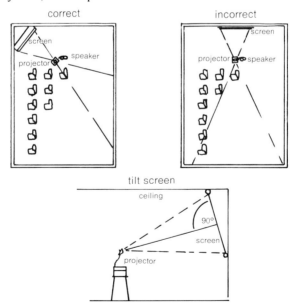

Because you are using this machine as an information transfer device, be sure all can see the screen clearly. By teaching from one fixed spot, you may block out much of the view for some students, so move around when the transparencies are in use so all can see the screen.

Many models of overhead projectors are available from $50 to $300, and all get the data in front of the group. It is not the unit, but how you use it that is important. I suggest placing your hand or pointer on the overhead projector itself, not on the screen, as you seek to emphasize a point. NOTE: *ALWAYS* have a spare bulb on hand for your unit! Overhead projector bulbs have a tendency to burn out at precisely the wrong time.

Place a table or desk beside the projector for the materials you will use during the class.

Registration Card

Each person ought to fill in some form of a registration card at the beginning of the first session. A sample registration card may look like this:

A G P READING REGISTRATION CARD

Name _____ Age _____ Years of Education _____
(Beyond Kindergarten)

Group _____ Instructor _____

1. _____ 2. _____ 3. _____

		Course Record—Words Per Minute			Minnesota Speed of Reading Test	
Session	Opening	Middle	End	Comprehension	Pre-Test (Form A)	Post-Test (Form B)
1					Correct _____	Correct _____
2					Rate _____	Rate _____
3						

How to figure:
1. Find the number of whole pages read and multiply by the words per page (WPP) figure for your book.
2. Add up the lines on the partial pages read and multiply by the words per line (WPL) figure for your book.
3. Add the WPP and WPL totals to get total words read.
4. Divide this total by the number of minutes read to get words per minute (WPM).

How to figure:
1. Determine the number of correct paragraphs. Put that in "correct" above.
2. Multiply that "correct" number by 50.
3. Divide that result by the number of minutes read (either 6 or 3). Put that number in "rate" above.

As the course proceeds each participant records on his card his reading rate on certain major timed drills and periodically notes his estimate of comprehension. All scores are recorded by the student himself. This relieves the teacher of that task, but also helps the student feel that he is in charge of his own success.

At the beginning of the first session, each class member should record some basic information on his card—name, age, years of education, group (there may be more than one group taught at a time), instructor. The blocks numbered 1, 2, 3 (to be discussed later in this book) are motivators to start each learner thinking about what it will be worth to him to work and to improve his reading. These cards ought to be collected by you at the end of each class session.

Redistribution of the cards to large classes for the second and third sessions can be eased by pre-sorting the cards into two, three or four groups, alphabetically by last names (A–G, H–N, O–Z, for example). Instruct your students to keep the cards moving around the room until each has found his own. If some haven't located their cards at the time of the first test, they can keep a record of their scores on a piece of paper and write them in on the card when they do receive it.

At the end of the course, you should ask the participants to respond to some evaluative questions on the back of the card. Encourage them to be candid about their feelings. These comments will help you evaluate your role in the class, and it is helpful in calling attention to areas where revisions may be needed in your program. Some suggested questions are given below.

1. How have you applied your new skills?
2. How will you apply them in the next 24 hours?
3. What was the one part of the course that had the greatest impact on your reading?
4. What is the one part of the course you would tell us to emphasize more?
5. What should we de-emphasize?
6. What would you improve about the instruction?
7. My quick overall evaluation of this experience is _____

Course Summary Sheet

Some form of a course summary sheet ought to be given to participants at the beginning of the first session to serve as a summary of the course content each week. The weekly summaries

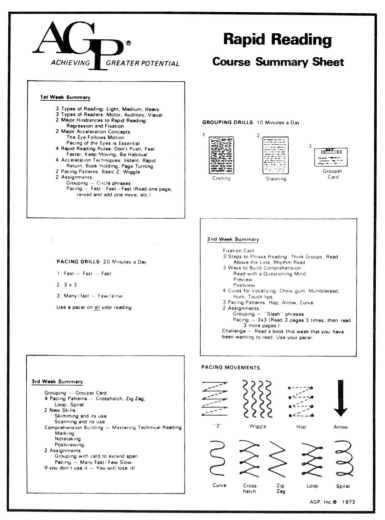

serve as a reminder of assigned drills and provide a quick review for the participants as the course progresses. This sheet also shows sample pacing patterns that will be learned in the course.

Practice Books

Before each session begins, the participants should select a practice book from the table. Since rapid reading is largely a matter of breaking old habits and forming new ones, light reading is called for until the new habits become established. Don't let your students concentrate too much on the technical content of a book until they have mastered the new reading *methods*. Works of fiction are ideal.

things to get ready   **39**

You will want to insure a wide variety of novels, suited to the various tastes of your class.

The books you choose should include several levels of difficulty so that your students can experiment with the various levels. It is not necessary that they know the difficulty level for every book, but you can tell them the approximate grade levels if they do ask. A formula for calculating the level of difficulty of any work is included later in this book.

Beware of books with language peculiarities, jargon and dialects, because these books are more difficult to understand and affect reading speed. *Huckleberry Finn*, for example, is an easy book made more difficult because of the dialect. You might include a limited number of such books in your selection, making sure that the majority do not have such language peculiarities. Class members have a tendency to concentrate on the unusual qualities in books at first.

In the course participants will want to figure how fast they were reading at various times. To assist in this you will need to calculate the words-per-line and words-per-page rates for each book. To do this, count the number of words in ten standard lines, and then divide by ten. This will give you the average words-per-line figure to calculate words-per-page. Write these scores inside the front cover. These are approximate rates, and participants should adjust their scores if their text contains many short lines.

Remember, the focus during class is on *principles* of reading, not on the *content* of the books. In order to get the principles learned, we suggest that you stay in the light novel-type books for class practice.

Grouper Card

The Grouper Card is a simple aid to the development of grouping skills. It is distributed after students begin developing their abilities to see more letters with each focus of the eyes. Participants are encouraged to use it as a drill at home. They will find newspapers especially useful with the Grouper, due to the narrowness of the columns.

The Grouper Card is designed so that the student can cut a small slot in the box at the top of the card, and attempt to read all the words in this slot at a single glance as he moves the card, not along the lines, but from line to line, straight down the page. The words in the slot on each line will be unrelated in meaning to the preceding

```
AGP    GROUPER

┌──┬──┬──┬──┬──┬──┐ (remove) ┌──┬──┬──┬──┬──┬──┐
└──┴──┴──┴──┴──┴──┘          └──┴──┴──┴──┴──┴──┘

1. Cut out center rectangle.
2. Guide grouper down center of page.
3. As eyes become accustomed to seeing all the words, extend
   the opening.

┌─────────────┬──┬──┬──┬──┬──┬─────────────┐
│  (remove)   │  │  │  │  │  │  (remove)   │
└─────────────┴──┴──┴──┴──┴──┴─────────────┘

1. Cut out end rectangles.
2. As you guide grouper down page, swing eyes from phrase to
   phrase.
3. Increase the size of the openings as you are able.
```

line's words. Participants may be a little confused by this at first, but will begin to move down the page at an increasingly rapid pace as their eyes get accustomed to the width of the slot.

Later, the double slots may be cut out and the Grouper Card used to develop eye-swing as the participant continues to practice his new skills. More will be said about this later in the book.

The Fixation Card

One of the best tools for helping students to understand how the eyes work and what fixation and regression are is the fixation card. This is simply a card or sheet of paper with several lines of print on it and with a hole through the middle of it.

While one person holds the card to his nose with the print side out he looks through the hole at the eyes of his partner who is reading aloud the print.

A G P FIXATION CARD

My school hood was a normal one, but I dropped out of high school three months before graduation because of death. My ambition in life has always been to be an accountant and play some kind of sport during the off season. After the death of my father our family grew from three children to the present eight children. Another goal is to be the greatest classical scholar, scientist, surgeon, movie star, and perhaps lover, that the world has ever known. I come from a very active family. ◯

My father says that your student body is composed of hippies, draft dodgers, free-love advocates and pleasure seekers. Please send me an application for admission. Can you mail it in a plain envelope and mark it personal? I have selected your college because of its superb academic program, its top-notch faculty, its intellectual atmosphere, also, my girlfriend has just been accepted for admission.

Now as one person reads the other person watches the eye movements. The eyes will move across the lines in a series of quick jerks called fixations. The task is to count the average number of fixations per line. Since each fixation represents a stopping of the eyes to focus on several characters on a line, we simply have to count the number of letters per line and then divide the total by the number of fixations for the line. The answer is the number of letters you can see per fixation—your span of perception.

But why read aloud? Because if we read silently, we are apt to cheat. We know there is someone looking through the card at us, and because we want to make a favorable impression on the other person, we tend not to fixate as often as we normally would. Instead, we glaze our eyes a little bit and sweep over the card without really reading. When you read aloud, you can't bluff. It will cause you to read slower, but you will still have the same fixation span. That part doesn't change; you simply spend a little bit longer on each span.

Rapid Reading Textbook

At the completion of a rapid reading course it is advisable to have some follow-up exercises for students to work on at home. One of the best ways to encourage this growth beyond the course is to provide the students with a review workbook. This rapid reading textbook may be given to participants at the close of the third class session for their continued review and skill development. There are many books available which include rapid reading exercises. You will want to browse in a bookstore and find one which you feel has the proper blend of rapid reading techniques and study skills. This will reinforce what you teach in class.

Two books are available which are based on the organization and methodology of rapid reading as it is discussed in this book. They are also written by the author of this text and will be complementary to what you teach in class. Needless to say, they are highly recommended. You ought to choose the book which best meets the needs of your particular students.

The instructional content is the same in both books, including a summary of the entire rapid reading course and then giving additional practice exercises and drills which go beyond the course and encourage long-term growth and reading efficiency. The difference between the books is in the emphasis of the readings included for practice and test purposes, and in the emphasis on specific kinds of reading. The two books are:

Learn to Rapid-Read, by Ben E. Johnson, Howard W. Sams & Company, Inc., 1973. This book is geared to the typical busy person, college or high school student, administrator, office worker, executive, tradesman, or simply the actively reading individual. It gives an insight into efficient reading habits and their application to studying, on-the-job reading requirements and leisure reading. The reading selections and tests are geared to an application of reading materials of a general and technical nature and are suitable for the general public.

Rapid Reading With A Purpose, by Ben E. Johnson, Regal Press, 1973. This book emphasizes reading materials which are religiously oriented, for people involved in various church-related activities. It will be of interest to students at religious high schools, colleges and seminaries, pastors, Sunday School workers, mission and denominational personnel, etc. The readings included in the book are taken from church-related and general religious publications so that practice and application are directed specifically toward church-related activities.

chapter 3
the content of class sessions

the content of class sessions

class sessions

This section outlines the actual teaching of a rapid reading course. These procedures are suggested as the guide for your rapid reading course because they have been carefully tested in hundreds of classroom situations around the country in the last several years and are designed to clearly and efficiently accomplish the goals of a good rapid reading course. You may feel at times that undue attention is devoted to relatively minor details, but remember that the intention is to prepare you as thoroughly as possible. You must be ready to handle the questions that will arise and to feel competent and thoroughly adequate to your responsibility as an instructor. At the end of this class session section, a list of commonly asked student questions, and their answers, is included. This will serve as a good review.

This section is divided into discussions of the three two-hour class sessions, and material is explained chronologically within each session. When certain procedures are repeated in two or three class sessions, the description of the first session's activities will be more lengthy and detailed than that of the succeeding sessions.

There is no lack of material for six hours of class time if the instructions are followed carefully. In fact, quite the opposite is true. We expect you to tailor the contents and the emphasis to meet the needs of your class. The two-hour class sessions are packed tightly, so work out carefully what you intend to say, and be sure you know *why* you want to say it!

You will sometimes find yourself rushing to finish on time. This is not harmful to the effectiveness of the class. It can create a positive attitude in the minds of your participants that the class is packed full of helpful information. But *never* sacrifice clarity of explanation in your haste to cover the material. Rather, when it is necessary to save time, diminish one or two five-minute timed tests to three or two minutes each.

You can enjoy teaching this course as it is laid out. You can make the class fun for yourself and for your participants. Use group dynamics to motivate your students. It isn't necessary or desirable to maintain a formal, quiet classroom atmosphere throughout the course!

Using your own personal teaching style, turn this into an enjoyable experience for your class members! Improving reading efficiency involves repetition and drills that aren't really fun, but your students will learn more and practice more when you make the class casually enjoyable as well as instructional.

Above all, keep the goal of rapid reading in mind: To learn the principles of reading improvement and the ways to apply the principles to personal needs and goals. Students are to develop efficient reading rates and a flexibility of reading so that they can adjust their speeds and style according to the difficulty of the material and the purpose for reading it. Your purpose is to guide and instruct in developing reading ability so they can make the new skills work to meet various reading needs.

session one

Prepare the room in advance of class time. Arrange the room for easy teaching and learning. You will find it helpful to have the registration card and course summary sheet distributed to the proper number of desks. This will help to avoid a widely scattered group. Class members will sit where the materials are.

Write a note on the chalkboard or on an easel at the front of the room, instructing each student to select a book (novel) from the table before the class begins.

1. *WELCOME THE CLASS TO RAPID READING.** (*Transparency #1*) Begin on time, introduce yourself and set the tone of the course. Tell the class a bit about yourself. Discuss the purpose for which the class has gathered—to improve reading efficiency in order to better meet the demands of required reading each participant has to face.

Involve your students in the discussion. Ask questions such as how many have had speedreading courses before, and under what circumstances. Inquire about their purposes in taking the course. "How many feel that this will be most helpful in your required reading? How many in your leisure reading? Any other kind?"

---

*Appendix A illustrates suggested content and design of the transparencies mentioned in the text. By referring to the appendix as you read you can see how these overhead projection transparencies can supplement and reinforce what the instructor is saying.

2. *REGISTRATION CARD.* (*Transparency #2*) Explain that this card is the record-keeper for each student's progress throughout the course. Have the class fill in the top section of the card. Then have them fill in the slots numbered #1, #2 and #3 with their answers to the following questions.

#1   How many hours a day (study day, work day, entire day) do you spend reading?

#2   How fast do you think you read now in light materials (novels)? (If a learner doesn't know how fast he reads, he probably doesn't know much else about his reading, and the recognition of this will motivate him to *want* to learn.) Since most will not know, have them guess so that they can compare later with their actual reading rate.

#3   What is your goal in the course? How fast (with normal comprehension) do you want to be able to read? Twice as fast? Three times as fast? 1000 wpm?

Transparency #3 stresses the point that this is a course in rapid reading, teaching not a single speed of reading for all materials, but an increased range of speeds. It is important for your students to keep in mind throughout the course that *their goal is flexibility of reading speeds* and not a superspeed.

Transparency #4 indicates that good study and learning habits form the basis for effective reading skills. Emphasize the "learning circle." Point out that as you increase reading speed, you must concentrate more. As you concentrate more you are certain to improve comprehension. If your comprehension is better, your retention of material is certain to be better. You now need to find out at what level their reading abilities are. You will administer two tests. One is an informal reading of a book, while the other is a formal standardized test.

3. *THE TIMED TESTS.*   First, ask your participants to find a convenient place to begin reading in their novels. Administer a five-minute timed test, using your stopwatch.

Instruct students *to read at their normal speed for normal comprehension.* This test will establish a baseline on which to build during the course and serve as a comparison score during the course.

Each person should calculate his own reading speed, using the instructions on the registration card and the WPP and WPL rates which you should have calculated and written in the front of each novel. This reading rate is entered in the "Session #1, Opening" box on the registration card.

Now ask some questions: How many are over 1,000 WPM? 750 WPM? 500? 250? (The majority of the class will be between 250 and 350 words per minute at this point.)

Now hand out a standardized reading test of your choosing, asking participants to keep the test face down on the desk. Read the instructions on the front page together. Instruct your class to read at their normal rate. Afterward, either have the students correct their own tests or collect them immediately. Inform the students that they will be given the same type of test at the conclusion of the course. One of the best standardized tests to use at this point is the Minnesota Speed of Reading Test. It only takes six minutes to administer. A list of Standardized Tests is located in Appendix C.

4. *THREE TYPES OF READING MATERIAL*. (*Transparency #5*) Because there are varying levels of reading, a rapid reading course stresses flexibility of reading. Speed decreases as the difficulty of reading material increases, but the techniques learned for raising speed in light material can be transferred to heavier materials, and with proportionate gains.

Since rapid reading is basically a matter of learning good reading habits and breaking old bad ones, light materials should be used in the rapid reading course in the beginning to make the building of new habits easier. The WPM rate from the first novel test is the present *top* speed, and this is what we will work on. As the *top* speed increases, speed in more difficult material will increase proportionately.

5. *PROBLEMS IN READING*. (*Transparency #6*) Show Transparency #6 to help your students gauge their individual levels of reading skill and to set a reasonable, achievable goal for *efficient* reading.

Readers commonly fall into three categories:

(a) The *motor reader* is still reading aloud (even though he may have his mouth closed) as he was taught to read in the elementary grades. He must use his motor skills: his tongue, his lips, his organs of speech, to form the words. This is called vocalizing. Since he forms the words as he reads them, he is limited to about 150 WPM, about the speed he can talk. He disturbs those around him as he says the words, and he tires easily because he works so hard at reading.

Here are two interesting points on vocalizing:

(1) The fastest speech on record was made by John F. Kennedy. The speech was short and emotional, averaging 337 words per minute, almost twice JFK's normal conversational rate.

(2) Children are taught to read aloud, and seldom receive training to read silently. This habit of forming words as we read them easily carries over to vocalizing. To demonstrate that vocalizing tendencies exist in almost all people, ask someone to silently count the number of students in the class, and he will very likely move his lips or whisper the numbers as he counts!

    (b) The *auditory reader* imagines (visualizes) or hears (verbalizes) each word as he reads and creates unnecessarily detailed mental pictures of the subject matter. He often concentrates so intently on each word that he can hear the words pronounced as he silently reads them. He achieves a reading speed up to about 300 WPM.

    (c) The *visual reader* is what you want your students to become. He passes the words directly from the page to the comprehension without any stops in between. He reads rapidly but efficiently and allows no wasted effort. These are efficient readers who can achieve higher speeds with proper training and practice.

Transparency #7 demonstrates the reading capabilities of each of these types of readers, and the class members may wish to find themselves on this chart.

You can lighten the mood a bit by referring to superspeeds of 15,000, 20,000 or 25,000 WPM which are advertized by some speedreading companies. Note that this is actually a rate that challenges the ability of the hand to turn the pages. Still, the point should be made that the brain is capable of almost unlimited speeds, and the participants should set their goals high.

Point out from *Transparency #7* that speed of reading varies according to the difficulty of the material, and emphasize that as words per minute increase in light reading, it will increase in the same proportion in medium and heavy reading. When WPM in light reading increases from 250 to 500, the WPM for heavy material will also double, perhaps from 100 to 200 WPM. *Note that the purpose of this course is to develop efficient reading rates and a flexibility so that each person is able to adjust his speed and style according to his material and his goal for reading it.*

6. *REGRESSION AND FIXATION.* (*Transparency #8*) Ask what kinds of things your participants think slow their reading. You will get answers such as noise, heat, poor vocabulary, drowsiness, illness, lack of interest (or too much interest), worry over personal problems, etc. All of these answers are correct, and can be classified as either internal distractions (worry) or external distractions (hot room).

Your students may have mentioned *re-reading* and reading *word-by-word*. These are two of the basic causes of slow reading—Regression and Fixation. Show *Transparency #8*. Make clear that fixation is a natural and necessary function because the eyes must stop to focus and to record symbols on the brain. *The problem comes in stopping too long on a word or words, and in stopping too often on a line.* The grouping exercises which follow later will remedy these inefficient habits. Many people think that their eyes can just flow down a page of print and that will bring efficient reading somehow. Well, that doesn't work.

To demonstrate this for themselves, suggest that each student try the "toothpaste test." He should stand in front of his bathroom mirror, put a dab of toothpaste on the two sides of the mirror, and then stand in front of it. Looking only at the toothpaste dabs, he should swing his eyes back and forth. The student will find that he cannot see himself clearly in the mirror as he moves his eyes between the dabs because his eyes have not stopped (fixated) to see himself in the mirror.

Show *Transparency #9*. Regression is the reversion of the eyes to words already read. This occurs especially with long words or unfamiliar words and concepts, and its detriment to rapid reading is obvious. If the eyes are flicking backwords, they will take much longer to move across the line. Make clear that regression is usually an unconscious act and is difficult to remedy unless the eyes are simply *forced* to move ahead consistently.

Now you are ready to introduce the most significant foundational principle of the course.

7. *THE EYES FOLLOW MOTION.* You can demonstrate the fact that eyes will always follow motion by making a quick movement at the periphery of someone's vision, and by noticing the

attention this attracts. Each member of the class surely has had the experience of being attracted by such a motion. You may want to note that many reading machines use a movement of some sort to force the eyes to keep moving. A good rapid reading course makes it all much simpler by *using the hand as a "pacer"* for the eyes. Now clinch your point by demonstrating the effect of a pacing motion.

Teach the Basic Z. Ask you students simply to duplicate on a page, as they read, the Z pattern outlined on *Transparency #11.*

Place your hand on the transparency, on the overhead projector, and trace the pattern on the page of print. Explain that the Basic *Z must be traced under each line, and that the Z pattern is stretched out on the transparency so it is easier to see.* They will always read every line. Students should be told simply to run their index finger along each line as they read, keeping their finger moving slightly ahead of their eyes so that the movement of the finger pulls the eyes steadily along the line, and back to the beginning of the next line again.

8. Now ask the students to find a good place to begin and to read in their books for five minutes. Remind them to *keep pacing* at all costs, even though the moving may be uncomfortable at first. Time the drill with your stopwatch.

When the five minutes have passed, give time to calculate speed. Then have some time for feedback. "How did you do? How many increased? Did any of you decrease? Why? How was your comprehension?"

Some will have slowed down slightly. Encourage them to try pacing themselves again. They'll increase as they get used to pacing. Resistance is not unexpected when trying something new and foreign to a lifetime habit!

Many will feel that their comprehension suffered a bit and you may explain that this is a natural result the first time pacing is tried, due to thinking more about the movement of the finger than the words on the page. Offer words of encouragement that this self-consciousness will soon disappear and comprehension will return to normal, while reading speed will continue to improve.

9. *TAKE A BREAK.* Let your participants stretch or go out for a drink of water. Be available to talk informally to any who appear interested. Don't let this go on for more than five minutes.

10. *WHAT ABOUT DETAILS?* When your participants return from the break, discuss with them how they feel about reading

with a pacer. They are probably worried that they will miss too much of a book's contents while reading faster. Assure them that details will fall into place as long as they emphasize major ideas.

Usually someone will question the use of rapid reading on reading they want to "savour," such as poetry. Assure them that such things should be read as slowly as necessary, at 50 or 60 WPM if their objective is to savor, and not to read it as rapidly as possible. Remind them that on any given page, a good visual reader may use three or four different speeds. Some reading, such as poetry, is meant to be read slowly and often aloud.

However, also point out that reading clinics have demonstrated that comprehension increases with rapidity of reading up to a point, simply because of the increased powers of concentration demanded of the rapid reader. In order to pace yourself as you read, you must *concentrate* more now on reading than ever before, thus increasing your awareness of what is being read. A positive attitude and a belief that you *can* read faster will help greatly in increasing speed.

11. *RULES FOR RAPID READING.* (*Transparency #12*) prepares the way to use the pacing technique most effectively. Your students should not feel *rushed*, but they should feel faster, an admittedly subjective achievement. Once more, emphasize the practice requirements. With strong attention to these rules, and with some additional tips, your students should improve their reading rates just a little bit more in the next five-minute test.

12. *ACCELERATION HELPS.* (*Transparency #13*) Just before the next five-minute test, discuss the four acceleration techniques shown on this transparency.

Indentation   Indent ¹/₂″ at the beginning and end of each line. Your students may wish to draw parallel lines down a page about a half inch in from each margin, and then practice reading between the lines. You will still see all of the words while looking at only 75% of the line. Since the average reader may take in 5–8 characters at each fixation, he doesn't need to start reading by focusing on the first letter of each line. If he indents a half inch, he will still see the first letter but will miss the margin. The same concept applies for the end of each line.

Lorem ipsum dolor sit amet, consectetur adipscing elit, sed diam nonnumy euusmod tempor incidunt ut labore et dolore magna aliquam erat volupat. Ut enim ad minim veniam, quis nostrud exercitation ullamcorper suscipit lab oris nisi ut aliquip ex ea commodo consequat. Duis autem vel eum irure dolor in reprehendert in voluptate velit esse molestaie consequat, vel illum dolore eu fugiat nulla pariatur. At vero eos et accusam et iusto odio blandit praesent luptatum delenit aigue duos dolor et molestias exceptur sint dupic non provident, simil tempor sunt in culpa qui deserunt mollit anim id est laborum et dolor fuga. Et harumd dereund facilis est er expedit distinct. Nam liber tempor cum nobis eligend optio comgue nihil impedit doming id quod maxim placeat facer possim omnis voluptas assumenda est, omnis dolor repellend. Temporibud autem quinusd at aur office debit aut tum rerum necessit atib saepe eveniet ut er repudiand sint et molestia non recus. Itaque earud reruam hist entaury sapiente delecatus auaut prefear enrdis doloribr asperibre repellat. Hanc ego cum tene sententiam, quid est cur verear ne ad eam non possing accommodare nost ros quos tu paulo ante cum memorie tum etia ergat. Nos amice et nebevol, olestias access potest fier ad augendas cum conscient to factor tum poen legum odioque cividua. Et tamen in busa neque pecun modut est neque nonor imper ned libiding gen epular religuard cupidat, quas nulla praid om umdant. Improb pary minuit, potius inam ut coercend magist and et dodecendesse videantur. Invitat igitur vera ratio ad bene anos ad iustitiam, aequitated fidem. Neque hominy infant aut inuiste fact et cond qui neg facile efficerd possit duo conetud notiner si effecerit, et opes vel fortunag vel ingen liberalitat magis conveniunt, da but tuntung et benevolent sib conciliant et, aptissim est ad quiet. Endium caritat praesert cum omning null sit cuas peccand quaert en imigent cupidat a natura facile explent sine julla inaura autend inanc sunt is parend non est nihil enim ad desidrabile. Concupis plusque in insupinaria detriment est quam in his et rebus emolument oariunt iniur. Itaque ne iustitial dem rect quis dixea per se ipsad optabil, sed quiran cunditat vel pluify. Nam dilig et carum esse est in propter and tuitior vitam et luptat pleniore efficit. Tia non ob ea solu quae egenium improb fugiendad improbitate putamuy sed mult etiam mag quod cuis. Guaea derata micospe rtiuneren guarent esse per sesars tam expendu quam nostros expetere quo loco visetur quibusing stabilit amicitaie atillard tuent amet eum locum seque facil, ut mihi detur expedium. It enim ritutes Lorem ipsum dolor sit amet, consectetur adipscing elit, sed diam nonnumy euusmod tempor incidunt ut labore et dolore magna aliquam erat volupat. Ut enim ad minim veniam, quis nostrud exercitation ullamcorper suscipit lab oris nisi ut aliquip ex ea commodo consequat. Duis autem vel eum irure dolor in reprehendert in voluptate velit esse molestaie consequat, vel illum dolore eu fugiat nulla pariatur. At vero eos et accusam et iusto odio blandit praesent luptatum delenit aigue duos dolor et molestias exceptur sint dupic non provident, simil tempor sunt in culpa qui deserunt mollit anim id est laborum et dolor fuga. Et harumd dereund facilis est er expedit distinct. Nam

Rapid Return — Don't allow the finger to dawdle on the return sweep. The eye is used to returning rapidly, and the hand should be pulled back to the beginning of the next line as rapidly as possible. Remember, now that you are indenting, your finger should return not to the first letter but to the indented beginning.

Book Holding — Hold the book from the top with the left hand, allowing your fingers to rest under the book. This allows you to turn the pages properly.

Page Turning   Use the index finger of the left hand to turn the pages from the top. This permits more efficient page turning and saves seconds each time a page is turned. Comprehension is improved because the distraction of page-turning is minimized.

NOTE: These book-holding and page-turning proce-
           dures will not work for your left-handed stu-
           dents. They should hold the book at the top
           with the right hand and turn pages with the
           thumb.

Give a five-minute timed test, making sure your participants use
the Basic Z and these techniques. The reading rate on this test
should be calculated and entered on the registration card.

13. GROUPING. (*Transparency #14*) This transparency
will provide an introduction to grouping by demonstrating that the
easiest and most natural way to read would be by phrases, not by
words. Show the transparency, and stand back and wait for your
students to realize that they have proven the point themselves!

The eyes must stop to see, so the issue is "what is the duration
of the stop, and how much do we see when we stop?"

Ask questions about Transparency #14 to make the point.
What is the difference between 13 stops or 13 words and five stops
or five phrases? What effect would cutting down from 13 to 5 stops
have upon your reading? Emphasize that we can double our speed if
we go the same rate and see twice as much at each stop!

Grouping is a key to comprehension! If the author thought
in phrases and wrote in phrases, how much more sense it makes
for us to read in phrases. Get reactions from your students on this
concept.

14. GROUPING DRILL I. (*Transparency #15*) Have your
class begin their grouping training by turning to the back of their
books and, in pencil, circle natural word groupings. Circles should
be in realistic word groups, approximately three per average line,
but this will vary with the size of the page.

Continue this circling for about a paragraph, focusing on the
circle instead of each particular word. Suggest that they use the
Basic Z pattern while reading the paragraph, using the forefinger to
hop from circle to circle. This should be practiced at home for ten
minutes each day for the coming week, until students begin to *think*
in terms of groups instead of word by word.

With practice, as grouping becomes natural, comprehension
increases. This occurs because reading groups of words most nearly

parallels the way in which the mind processes information, by taking in concepts rather than individual words. This underscores the importance of faithful practice of the grouping drills.

15. *PACING MOTION—WIGGLE.* (*Transparency #16*) Use this transparency to show the variety of movements, and to show that the first pattern has already been learned.

Point out to your students that there are three basic pacing motions:

a. across the page—Basic Z
b. down the page—Wiggle
c. rhythm reading—Hop

The other six pacing motions which are suggested during the course are called comfort patterns because they provide a variety from which the students may choose two or three which they prefer and find more comfortable to use.

Demonstrate the Wiggle, *Transparency #17.*

Allow time for experimentation with the Wiggle even though it may seem awkward. This is a rhythmic, gentle back-and-forth motion which emphasizes down-the-page movement.

You may have had comments about the Basic Z being "too much motion." The Wiggle is much less action on the page, but still moves across the line and down the page. Remember, *the hand is supposed to pull the eyes along the lines so make certain that you remind students to never let the eyes move opposite the direction the hand is moving.*

After your class members have gotten the idea of this pacing motion on a page of their book, administer a three or five minute test using this pattern. Allow time at the end for calculation of speed. Engage in some quick feedback. "Any of you prefer this over the Basic Z? Why?"

16. *PACING DRILL I.* (*Transparency #18*) Explain the Fast-Fast-Fast drill, and the need for practicing during the week. The Fast-Fast-Fast can be practiced in class for a few minutes, depending on the time remaining.

Fast-Fast-Fast: Read page one very rapidly while de-emphasizing comprehension. Stop at the end of page one. Repeat page one and proceed rapidly to the end of page two. Return to page one and read rapidly moving on to the end of page three. Repeat this procedure, each time adding an additional page! The repetition will cement the learning of pacing.

1. Read page 1 as fast as possible. (Don't worry about comprehension.)

2. Re-read page 1 rapidly and move on to page 2, still reading rapidly.

3. Repeat pages 1 and 2 and add page 3, etc.

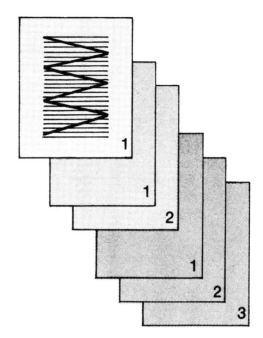

Ask the class to drill in this manner at home this week, for 20 minutes each day. This drill stresses development of the habit of pacing so that it will become natural and comfortable.

Why this drill? Illustrate with the principle of over-training. A dash man who wants to feel comfortable at 100 yards will sprint 440 yards every day. A miler runs for 5–10 miles a day. If you are up to 500 WPM now and feel uncomfortable, the principle is to get up to 750, so 500 will seem like coasting.

This Fast-Fast-Fast drill will improve eye-hand coordination so that regression is not as likely, and your students will be confident and comfortable at speeds greater than their present level. Encourage them to try it—we know it works—but they need to experience it to convince themselves.

17. *FINAL TIMED TEST.* Ask students to choose one of the two movements they have learned, and to read using it for five minutes. Before you give the "start" signal, review the rules (Transparency #12) and remind them to turn pages with the left

hand. After five minutes, have each participant calculate his score and enter it on his registration card. Also ask each person to estimate his comprehension rate as excellent, normal, fair or poor, and enter that as well. If time permits, ask for some quick feedback.

18. *SUMMARY. Transparency #19* will remind the students of the material covered in this first session.

19. *Transparency #20* will urge them to practice for success: Grouping—10 minutes per day, Pacing—20 minutes per day.

20. Collect the registration cards and have your participants leave the books where you can easily collect them for the next class session.

session two

1. *WELCOME AND REVIEW.*   Be friendly, warm and per-sonable in opening the second session, perhaps expressing a tongue-in-cheek assurance that the class members spent all their waking hours in drilling for rapid reading. You may want to ask how many used their new skills to good advantage during the week, and in what way. Did they try pacing on any non-fiction? With what results?

Then review quickly the contents of Session One, using *Transparency #19.*

For a more thorough review you may want to show *Transparencies #18* and *#12.*

Then remind the class, with *Transparency #16,* of the two pacing motions learned in the first session. Inform them that the next three pacing motions will be learned in this class.

As an encouragement and positive reinforcement, you might briefly cite some of the statistical results of the first session: average class beginning speed, average class ending speed, percentage of increase, or perhaps highest WPM achieved by a class member.

Give an overview of this session's contents. *Transparency #21* will provide a context for activities in this session.

2. *THE INITIAL TIMED TEST.*   Give a five-minute drill in the book chosen by each student, with each one choosing his favorite of the first two pacing drills. Allow time to calculate scores and to record them.

Have a little feedback from the group: "Are you still improving? Is your self-consciousness about the pacing motion diminishing? How is comprehension?"

3. *FIXATION CARD.* First review the concept of fixation as explained in the first session. State that it will be interesting to find out how many fixations each person makes on a single line, and for that purpose the Fixation Card is necessary. Participants will work in pairs on this, one reading the copy on the card aloud while the other peers through the hole at the reader's eyes and counts the number of fixations the eyes make on each line. Each fixation will appear as a slight jerk of the eyes.

When the first reader is finished and the average number of fixations per line has been calculated, the procedure is reversed and the second person reads aloud while his partner counts his eye-stops. Your students will wonder if reading aloud increases the number of fixations per line. The answer is no. The eyes will have the same number of fixations as when they are reading silently, but the eyes will be fixating on each word for a slightly longer period of time.

Ask the class for the average number of fixations for the various members. You can tell them that the optimum number on this length is three (2" per fixation on a 6" line). *Five, six or seven stops per line will be average.* By simple division, counting the number of characters per line and then dividing by the number of fixations for that line, your students can tell how many characters they are taking in with each fixation. Your students can then see how far they must improve their eye-span and the need for the grouping drills to develop eye-span.

This is a good warming up and loosening up exercise for the class early in the session. Not only will students learn from this, but they will have fun with it.

4. *RETEACH GROUPING.* (*Transparency #22*) Give the three steps to developing the student's ability to see large groups of words: group words, soft focus, rhythm read.

Using the transparency, point out that the problem in learning to see a widened span of letters is not so much a physical problem as it is a psychological problem. We are not conditioned to *think* in terms of clusters of letters. Instead we are conditioned to think in terms of just a few letters per fixation. Students must be encouraged to "think groups."

Next, emphasize the soft focus concept and have your class practice it on a page to get the feel of it. "Soft focus" is simply relaxing the eyes so that a wider span of vision is possible. Most of us read with a "hard focus," an intense stare at each word. Soft focus is relaxed focus, a kind of daydreaming stare which attempts to look slightly above the line rather than directly at the words. It is a kind of reading between the lines. Have them try this for several days and they will see that their peripheral vision widens.

5. *GROUPING DRILL II.* (*Transparency #23*) Class members are now ready for the second week's grouping drill. Have the class put slashes in a paragraph or two at the top of a page in their books. Instruct them to read and re-read this passage, attempting to read all the words between the slashes in one fixation. Then encourage them to read and re-read the whole page. The newly developed habit will carry over from the slashed portion to the balance of the page and reinforce the exercise. A pacing motion should be used while practicing the drill.

6. *TEACH THE HOP. Transparency #24* demonstrates the Hop. The Hop helps the eyes fixate on groups of words. The finger points at the line you are reading in two or three places with a rapid hopping movement. A one-finger Hop is not unlike the Basic Z in form, except that it is easier and faster than sliding the finger in a Z pattern, and does not permit the eyes to fixate on every word on a line, while adding the element of rhythm to reading. Some might try spreading two fingers in a V pattern and try a two-finger Hop to reduce the amount of motion, yet still pull the eyes across the line and down the page. Combining the Hop and soft focus may really be the key that unlocks the door to comprehension for many of your participants.

At this point some participants may bring up the fact that they find themselves "reverse reading," that is, reading the next line as they sweep their eyes back to the left hand side of the page. Encourage those who find they are "reverse reading" that it is beneficial to their reading, and they may in fact want to practice and develop this ability *after* they have developed the skills taught in this course. Assure the other students that this is not expected of them and it is not even desirable unless it is a natural, automatic process.

7. *COMPREHENSION BUILDING.* Ever since the beginning of the course, perhaps first at the time you taught the Basic Z,

you have been stressing that students should not rush faster than their ability to comprehend. "Read no faster than *normal* comprehension" should be your constant admonition to the class.

You can stress this point by asking if anyone ever has trouble with his mind wandering as he reads, or with daydreaming between lines. The problem here is that the mind, which is fully capable of comprehending at a very rapid pace, is processing information faster than the eyes' ability to send messages to the brain.

The aim of a good rapid reading course is to narrow this gap, so that the mind has no chance to relax and wander while the eyes catch up. This means that rapid reading techniques, when practiced conscientiously, will increase concentration. Increased efforts at concentration must begin.

COMPREHENSION BUILDER I—Read With a Questioning Mind. It is still possible to read a passage and miss its contents if it is approached improperly. The proper way to get the meaning from any passage is not with a *passive* but with a *questioning mind.* *Transparency #25* asks the questions of WHO—WHAT—WHERE—HOW—WHEN—WHY.

The reader should ask himself these questions just a moment before each drill to prepare the questions in his mind. As this becomes habitual, more specific questions can be asked on the basis of reading a book's introduction, table of contents, and based on what is already known about the subject. When the reading is finished each person should try to answer each question in his mind.

Illustration: As a college professor I used to assign my classes a reading section and say, "I will ask you questions at the end of the reading." But, after awhile I switched to asking questions of the students before they read, such as, "As you read, find the three major themes of the author." What is the difference for the students? The questioning mind is "in gear" *during* the reading, as opposed to idling until later, not knowing what the questions would be. This way the students read for answers and don't merely turn pages. It is the difference between a passive reader—one who simply wants to complete the reading, and an active reader—one who wants to find information.

Your participants may be interested in knowing that concentration automatically declines toward the bottom of each page thus causing comprehension to be better toward the top of a page, and worse toward the bottom. You can interject this information if you wish. A detailed explanation of this fact can be found in the Reading Tests section, entitled "How to Construct Your Own Test."

COMPREHENSION BUILDER II—Previewing. *Transparency #26* acquaints the reader with the subject matter before beginning actual reading and increases comprehension because he knows what to expect as he reads. It can be compared to reading a road map before beginning a journey. This gives an overview of the trip before beginning the driving. This way any obstacles or surprises are discovered before you read them. To preview a book, read:

> *Book Covers*—Often exerpts from reviews are printed on the book cover. You may not agree with the reviewer, but he will generally give an insight into the high points of the contents of the book.
>
> *Table of Contents*—Many books include a detailed table of contents which lists in outline form the points and sub-points of the work. This is the closest thing to an outline of the book that you can get. It is a good place to get an overview of content.
>
> *Introduction*—Here the author states his reason for writing the book, the need he wishes to meet and his method for accomplishing his goals.
>
> *Diagrams, Charts, Maps*—These highlight major points covered in the text in a visual manner. If it is important enough to highlight or illustrate it is important enough to look at a second time.

These techniques will give an idea of the thesis or direction of the book. They can be adjusted to your various reading needs. The point is that you familiarize yourself with the contents *before* you actually read so your mind will feel as if what you are reading is familiar and be freed to sort out and analyze what you read.

You can't *make* anyone learn, but by your attitude you set the learning environment for your class. You are trying to change behavior that is firmly entrenched, and it will take your skill to put across the motivation to develop the skills. Try to stay "learner oriented" by letting each member of your class experience each step while you stay expectantly positive.

8. *MIDDLE READING TEST.* Test the class for five minutes in their novels. Before beginning reading, use Transparency

#25 again to trigger questions. Encourage participants to raise questions over what they are about to read. Each student should use his favorite pacing pattern. After the test, have each student calculate his score and record it. Remind class members that you are trying to build comprehension. State that you expect "normal" comprehension.

9. *TAKE A BRIEF BREAK.*

10. *VOCALIZING.* Some members of your class have become aware that they have a vocalizing problem. To insure that all your students discover if they have this tendency, instruct your class to read a short paragraph silently, holding a hand on the throat or lips while reading. Any motion detected indicates vocalizing. You might also ask them to silently count the number of people in the room, and then while they are counting ask them if they are moving their lips. Most will be. This is a good illustration of vocalizing.

For those few who find they vocalize while reading, show *Transparency #27* and explain the simple (and lighthearted) steps to overcome it: Chew Gum, Mumbleread, Touch Lips, Hum. Rhythmic, hearty gum chewing while reading keeps the reader from forming words while reading.

To "Mumbleread" is to repeat aloud a nonsense word or two while reading; to "touch lips" is simply a means of retaining consciousness of the vocalizing problem. You might add that it is best to touch one's own lips, not those of a friend! Humming also prevents lip movement. The object of these exercises is simply to get participants to focus attention on their vocalizing tendencies so that they will be conscious of the problem and attempt to stop vocalizing.

11. *PACING DRILL II. Transparency #28* will explain the "3 × 3" drill, used to break old habits and establish better ones. Participants are to practice this drill for 20 minutes each day at home this week. Essentially, this drill involves reading 3 pages 3 times. Each time that the same three pages are read the reader will speed up slightly because the pages are familiar.

3 Times 3: Read three pages for normal comprehension. Stop. Go back and repeat those same three pages two more times. On the third time through add three more pages. Re-read those three pages two more times. Continue adding three pages at a time and reading them three times.

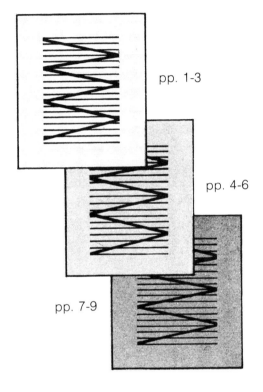

pp. 1-3

pp. 4-6

pp. 7-9

1. Use a pacing motion.

2. Read 3 pages. Stop. Repeat the same 3 pages at a slightly faster rate.

3. Repeat the same 3 pages for the third time reading as rapidly as possible.

4. On the third time through, do not stop, but let your momentum carry you through.

5. Repeat the process.

The repetition of this drill also helps to build comprehension, because it once again raises the comfort level and helps the student to be less aware of the pacing hand.

12. *ARROW PACING PATTERN. Transparency #29* will illustrate the Arrow Pacing motion. This technique can be used several ways:

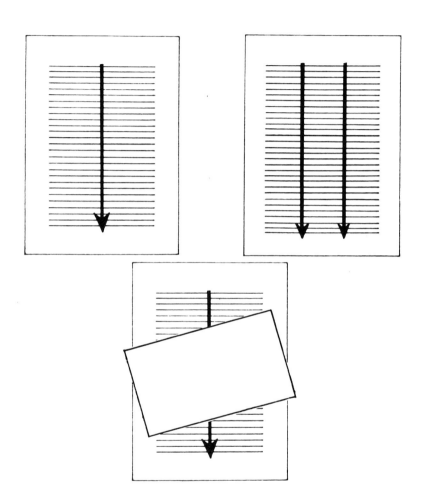

A. the finger can be moved down the middle of the page;
B. or down either the left or right edge;
C. or by using two fingers in a V shape to provide two focal points for the eyes;
D. or by moving the entire hand or a card down the page. When using a card, it is helpful to tilt the card slightly lower on the left, so that as the reader completes one line his eyes follow the slant of the card to the beginning of the next line. This also creates a left-to-right pacing movement.

Try a quick three-minute drill with this motion, and re-emphasize the proper method of turning a page.

13. *PREVIEW EXERCISE.* (*Transparency #30*) Have each person switch his book with a neighbor so that each person has a different book, and challenge each person to skim the entire book in five minutes, using the Arrow. This motion will be especially useful in this exercise. Emphasize that the students will have to keep those pages turning to get through the book in the alloted time.

After the time is up, get some feeiing from the class as to how much of the contents they were able to pick up in just five minutes. They will remember names, dates, places, recurring phrases. Stress that if they spend three or four times as long, say *fifteen* or *twenty* minutes to preview each book they read, and then re-read using the pacing motions and giving particular attention to comprehension, they will find that their speed and retention will increase dramatically and the time spent will be much less than that usually spent in "digesting" a book in one slow reading.

This can be demonstrated by having the class begin reading from the beginning of the book just previewed, for about three minutes, using their favorite pacing motions. Their speed and comprehension should show uniform improvement.

From this point on, participants should be encouraged to *always* PREVIEW when they read, even in class drills. Be sure to allow a minute or two for this purpose before beginning future timed drills.

14. *COMPREHENSION BUILDING.* Have the participants work in pairs. Each should read for about three minutes in his book, making sure it is material just previewed, starting at a good transitional point. Then each one should exchange his book with his partner, beginning where his partner began the first time, and read the same material, again for three minutes. Emphasize that each should use his most comfortable pacing method and work for both

speed and comprehension, asking those key questions about the book: WHO, WHAT, WHERE, HOW, WHEN, WHY.

After the three minutes is up and each has read the same material, turn them lose for about three minutes to discuss, as partners, the contents of the two passages read. Suggest that they ask each other the questions just discussed, checking each other's answers by their own knowledge of the material. This method of articulating a book's contents is a highly efficient study skill and one that students should consider to make productive use of in their study time.

15. *CURVE PACING MOTION.* The smoothness and naturalness of the Curve, without jerky starts and stops, appeals to some.

Transparency #31 demonstrates this motion. Give it a three-minute try and get reactions compared to the other motions that have been learned so far. Advantages? Disadvantages?

Your class should be interested to know that pacing keeps the reader more attentive and alert by keeping him physically involved. It is very difficult to fall asleep while pacing! And when the eye-hand coordination of pacing becomes a natural sequence, reading speed and comprehension increase.

Suggest that the class members try another approach to pacing by turning the pacing hand to rest on the heel and moving only the index finger to pace. This alternative keeps the hand relaxed when pacing for a long period of time.

16. *REVIEW.* End the class with a review. Why do we pace? Why do we group? Why do we use our hand and finger? How is comprehension related to speed? Any other why, how, what, when questions to build comprehension in your learners of what they are learning!

17. *FINAL TIMED TEST.* Have each participant choose any of the motions that they have been learning (using *Transparency #17* for review). Review the tips and hints for speedier reading, including the concept of Previewing. In addition, explain that you would like each student to be able to write that comprehension was "normal" in the comprehension slot at the end of this drill. *Therefore they must slow down if necessary, while aiming at normal comprehension.*

After the five minute test, have your students calculate their scores, and give an estimate of comprehension.

You should expect scores to drop a bit, but you will still find significant increases over the beginning speeds in the first session, and most likely with improved or normal comprehension.

18. *SUMMARIZE.* Use *Transparency #21* to review the session's activities. Review the drills that are to be practiced: Grouping, 10 minutes per day, Pacing, 20 minutes per day.

Send the participants away with a few words of encouragement. As a parting shot, challenge each one to rapid read one book this week that he would not normally have read. The sense of achievement will be a strong reward and reinforcement.

Collect your record cards; retain the practice books.

session three

1. *WELCOME AND REVIEW.* Once again begin with a few friendly words, perhaps a question or two about the class members' experience of the past week, and a note of positive encouragement. *Transparency #19* will review the first session's activities.

Transparency #21 will review the second session.

Transparency #32 will give an introduction to this session's activities. You might ask how many took up the challenge to read one extra book this past week, and congratulate any who did.

2. *FIRST TIMED TEST.* To get things rolling, you may wish to review *Transparency #12* and the rules for rapid reading.

Then have each participant choose one of the pacing motions from *Transparency #16.* The class will read for five minutes, and then calculate and record scores in the box marked "*opening, Session 3.*"

Have as much interaction with the class as possible to establish a friendly atmosphere for the session.

3. *GROUPING DRILL III.* Review the concept of grouping. Why do we group? To stop word-by-word reading and to increase the number of words seen per eye fixation. Review the drills already covered, and introduce the Grouper Card (*Transparency #33*).

The Grouper Card helps to accustom the eyes to read increasingly larger groups of words. Pull the card down the page as quickly as possible while the eyes fixate on each line. Content of the reading material is not important here, just the fact that the words visible are read as a group.

First try the card down the page, seeing parts of words. When the student can clearly see the letters at the edges of the cut, he is ready to cut out another $^1/_4''$ and try that. Later, try cutting both blanks at the bottom of the card, hopping the eyes from group to group as you slide it down the page. As it gets easier and easier to see the two groups on one line, widen the slots toward the middle until the entire line is visible.

These exercises with the Grouper Card are to be practiced for ten minutes each day for the coming week.

Now summarize grouping, noting that all reading programs emphasize this principle, and that the eyes are able to grasp phrases rather than words when serious practice is applied and the ability to group is developed.

4. *CROSSHATCH, ZIGZAG PACING MOTIONS. Transparency #34* illustrates the Crosshatch, which can be used with either one or two fingers. Have your class try this for a timed drill of three minutes. At the end of the time, show *Transparency #25* and again discuss level of comprehension.

After hearing their reactions to this motion, use *Transparency #35* to teach the Zigzag, and follow the usual procedure. This motion has an advantage in cutting down through the lines and is very useful for skimming and scanning.

5. *PACING DRILL III.* Review the pacing drills already covered, using *Transparency #16.*

Introduce *Transparency #36*, the Many Fast/Few Slow drill. Practice this in class for a few minutes, using one of the last two pacing motions.

Many Fast/Few Slow: Read many pages (a chapter, 25 pages, etc.) very rapidly (pp. 1–25). Go back and re-read a few pages very slowly and for total comprehension (pp. 1–5). At the end of a few pages speed up and read many pages very rapidly again (pp. 6–25). Stop. Go back and read slowly again for a few pages (pp. 6–10). Speed up, and so on. Read many pages fast and a few slow.

Essentially, each person is to read many pages very quickly (preview) and then go back over them slowly. This drill stresses both speed and comprehension. It is to be practiced for 20 minutes each day for the coming week.

1. Read many pages
   very rapidly.

2. Repeat the first few
   pages reading for
   comprehension.

3. Begin reading many
   pages again, very
   rapidly, adding a
   few pages.

4. Repeat a few pages
   again, reading for
   comprehension.

5. Continue, repeating
   steps 3 and 4.

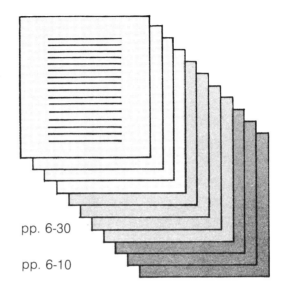

pp. 6-30

pp. 6-10

6. *SKIMMING & SCANNING.* (*Transparency #37*) One of the most valuable things you will teach is the difference between skimming, scanning and reading, and when each can contribute to a reader's successful ability to gather information from the written page. What is the difference between skimming and scanning?

Skimming—Skimming is defined as reading unfamiliar material, looking for main ideas. When you skim you rapidly perceive the main ideas of a book, chapter, report or article instead of reading the material from beginning to end. But skimming involves more than just lightly passing your eyes over the pages in hopes that something is going to hit you.

So how do you skim? Develop the habit of rapidly reading the first sentence of each paragraph which is nearly always the topic sentence (the sentence which spells out the most important point in the paragraph). This will enable you to have a basic understanding of the important ideas in the work, at a speed five or six times as fast as you normally could read the material. As you rush through the work skimming, don't allow yourself to read the details of any paragraphs, only topic sentences. You are reading for ideas now, not details.

This technique is useful in gathering major ideas on specific subjects from new material, such as in doing research before writing a paper or in determining if a book is worth reading.

Scanning—This technique is useful in locating specific facts in material that has already been read.

Scanning is defined as reading familiar material, looking for facts or details.

If you are reading for details, the scanning technique will be a great aid to you. It will allow you to quickly find specific points, or to locate facts and figures to support an idea. Scanning is like skimming in its visual gliding through reading material. Yet, it is different in two ways: first it helps the reader find information that he already knows is in the work (because he has already read the material). Secondly, the reader must know what he is looking for.

You will find that items you are looking for seem to stand out at you as you scan. Any items concealed in a paragraph—such as dates, titles, key words, places, vocabulary, and technical facts— can easily be found by scanning. Simply run your eyes in diagonal lines from the first word in a paragraph to the middle line of the paragraph at the right margin and then back to the beginning of the second paragraph. Repeat this technique for each paragraph. When you scan you program your mind to find your word or phrases by making yourself very conscious of the word you are looking for, and it fairly leaps out at you when you come near it. By heightening your awareness of a word, you have made it easier to perceive when you get near it.

Reading—Rapidly seeing every word on the page; comprehending what is being said and meant.

When are these techniques helpful? Most busy people use skimming as an aid to reading. Skimming enables a person to get a good idea of what a work is about even though not having time to read the entire work. When trying to decide if an article or paper should be read, skimming can be useful as a timesaver. It helps a reader decide what *not* to read.

To illustrate the usefulness of scanning, request each person to choose a word which occurs frequently in his novel (suggest "their" if class members cannot think of a specific word). Instruct the class to use the scanning technique to zigzag through each page to find that word. Give a signal to start and call out five-second intervals ("5 sec., 10 sec., etc.").

Each participant is to note the nearest interval of seconds when he finds his word, and then he calculates his WPPM (words *passed* per minute) score using the WPM calculations method. Your class will be amazed at how quickly they spotted their words, and also at the number of words passed per minute.

7. *MIDDLE TIMED TEST.* Give a five-minute test, each person using his favorite pacing motion. Give time to calculate and record the score. Remind the class to preview before giving the start signal.

8. *TAKE A BREAK.*

9. *LEARNING SKILLS.* Now show the relationship between learning and rapid reading. First emphasize that rapid reading is enhanced by the practice of good learning skills. Without effective study techniques, the best reading ability won't accomplish the studying task facing most people today. Much precious time is wasted when readers "read" material without mastering the contents. Learning skills incorporated with effective reading skills make an unbeatable combination.

Following are general steps which aid in mastering and retaining contents. Each step takes a little time and effort, but saves time in the long run. The four steps are:

READ	Prior previewing and a careful rapid reading get the reading accomplished efficiently.
COMPREHEND	Approach the material with a questioning mind. After each section, tell yourself your understanding of the essence of what you read, or even state it in writing.
RETAIN	The key to effective memory is recitation and frequent review using minimal notes. Discuss with yourself the contents just read.
INTEGRATE	Ponder the material and consider its implications in light of what you already know and your reason for reading it.

10. *LOOP AND SPIRAL PACING MOTIONS.* Both are variations of the Basic Z for smoothness and comfort.

The Loop (*Transparency #38*) tends to take the eyes in a rhythmic pattern that is very pleasing to some people. As the finger loops up and back down, the eyes take a glance at old material, which can be reassuring to a reader trying pacing as a new skill.

The Spiral (*Transparency #39*) is another comfort pattern. The smoothness and rhythm attract some people, and your job is to get each student to try it.

11. *COMPREHENSION BUILDER III.* (*Transparency #40*)

A. *Notetaking.* How do your students take notes? Most people take them with the idea of reading them "later on," but never really do it. Or they underline so much of a book that it has to be completely reread.

Using the page of print (*Transparency #10*) put a felt-tip pen between the 2nd and 3rd fingers of your pacing hand. Now every time you read a statement that your would ordinarily underline, don't! Instead roll your hand over and dot the margin opposite the statement while hardly skipping a beat of pacing. The advantages to this system are extensive.

First of all, reading is not interrupted by the act of underlining, thus your concentration is not broken, thereby losing comprehension. When a person goes back to evaluate the dots he has made, he automatically reviews the material, and at this time he may underline the most important points. When he goes back later to review the book, he automatically has major points (underlined) and sub-points (dotted but not underlined), and his review becomes much more effective.

B. *Postviewing.* After reading an article, book or other reading material, and having dotted the margins, we now suggest going back to postview these dotted areas. With the overall view and comprehension you have of the main thrust of the author's thinking, you can underline, redot in another color, or sideline a passage to highlight it.

In our experience a person can preview, rapid read and postview with greater comprehension and in a shorter time than an old-style normal reading would take.

12. *FINAL TIMED TESTS.* Review any material which might be helpful in building speed.

A. Give the final five-minute test in the novel. Class members should choose the motion that is most effective for them, and should aim vigorously for good speeds and *normal* comprehension.

The score for this test should be entered in the box marked *End, Session 3*, and should be followed by a comprehension estimate.

One of the following four words should be placed in the comprehension box:

EXCELLENT—NORMAL—FAIR—POOR

B. Hand out the standardized test of your choice and give the test in the same way as was done in the first session.

13. Ask your participants to turn their record card over and to answer the questions on the reverse side as fully as possible. Their responses are helpful in evaluating the effectiveness of the course in general and teachers are always interested in comments about their teaching.

14. *CONCLUDE ON A POSITIVE NOTE!* Review the contents of the three sessions briefly: *Transparency #19, Transparency #21*, and *Transparency #32*.

Remind the class that there are seven days of practice to go. They are to spend ten minutes each day on the grouping drill and twenty minutes on pacing.

THE COURSE IS NOT OVER!

Transparency #41 states that the benefits are still to come. Stress that each person will have to work at his new skills to keep them sharp and useful. Motivate the class members to an enthusiasm to continue to use and develop their skills. Tell them a bit about the textbook on rapid reading (if you use one) and encourage them to use it as the basis for their continued skill development and follow-up. Send them away with a feeling that they have learned a valuable skill that will make a real difference in their reading and study habits.

Collect the registration cards, instruct the students to leave the books, pass out the rapid reading textbooks.

questions frequently asked in rapid reading classes

Most teachers of rapid reading quickly learn that the questions participants ask are not really very difficult to answer once the teacher is familiar with the basic concepts of rapid reading instruction.

Pacing

1. What happens if I stop using a pacer?

   Nothing, right away. Gradually you will lose speed and comprehension as you fall back into old patterns of reading. The eyes must be constantly paced forward.

2. What if my finger seems to slow me down?

   Practice more; try a different pacing pattern.

3. Can I substitute anything for my pacing finger?

   Yes, outside of class you can use anything you want—pencil, card, ruler, etc. It is the motion that is important.

4. How much time should I spend practicing the reading techniques?

   A minimum of thirty minutes each day.

5. Can I practice the reading techniques on textbooks or technical reading?

   Yes, definitely.

6. I'm reading the second line backwards—is that good?

   It is if you do it with ease. It is called reverse reading, and not everyone can do it.

7. What simple techniques will facilitate pacing?

   Book holding, indentation, page turning, rapid return.

8. Should my eyes be following my hand?

   No, your eyes should follow the lines of print. The eyes are attracted in regular, steady patterns by the motion of the pacing pattern.

9. Since I'm the only one who likes the loop pacing pattern, what does this mean?

   Nothing of significance, except that you like the loop!

10. I lose enjoyment. How can I read and enjoy what I'm reading at high speeds?

    If your purpose is enjoyment, read for that purpose and slow down.

Grouping

1. I'm still reading word-by-word. What should I do?

    Practice more. The time it takes to learn grouping varies from person to person.

2. I'm still vocalizing. What should I do?

    Set a time each day to practice the vocalizing cures.

    Spend as much time as necessary to cure yourself.

3. What is soft focus again?

    Reading between the lines with a relaxed gaze.

4. How long should my word groups be?

    Varied lengths, but no longer than practical. Challenge yourself to slightly longer groups all the time.

Comprehension

1. Will the principles of rapid reading work on everything?

    Yes, but not everything will be read at the same rate.

2. How fast should I read?

    No faster than normal comprehension.

3. After one week I'm not satisfied with my comprehension. What should I do?

    Stop stressing speed and work on raising comprehension; slow down.

4. How do I know that speed increase is really double and not just skimming?

    Test yourself to see if you know what you read. Have someone else question you.

5. How do I know that the standardized tests (Pre and Post) are equal in difficulty?

    You'll have to take our word and that of the test for it. Switch the order and give the Post-test first if you have any doubts.

6. What is the relationship between retention and reading time?

    See the *Ebbinghaus Curve* in this book.

General

1. Everyone reads faster than I do. Why?

    I'm not certain they do. If so, perhaps it takes you a little longer to learn these skills, but you will probably have high comprehension.

2. How does this program compare to the Evelyn Wood program, or others like it?

    Basic differences: (1) cheaper, (2) shorter time, (3) we teach reading principles applicable to all kinds of reading, they teach specific application of techniques to various kinds of reading, i.e., how to read a newspaper, how to read a novel, etc., and (4) we do not push for super speeds.

3. How fast do *you* read?

   In what? I won't tell (until after the course).

4. How fast will *I* read?

   At least twice as fast as you do now.

5. How fast do most people read upon completion?

   About three times faster, approximately 900 words per minute.

6. Can I repeat the course a second time?

   Yes.

7. How do you figure words per line?

   Count words in three lines; divide by three.

8. What about cheating on reading tests?

   Why cheat?

9. What is an Efficient Reading Rate?

   A reading rate which maximizes the identifying and absorbing of details and ideas in light of the reader's purpose.

10. What is vocalization?

    Pronouncing words, silently or aloud, when reading. The lips, tongue or vocal cords are active.

11. What is subvocalization?

    The lips, tongue or vocal cords do not move, and yet inner speech (word thinking) exists.

chapter 4
helpful things to be aware of

helpful things to be aware of

This chapter includes an assortment of information which will enrich your teaching of rapid reading.

research on the teaching of reading

The following pages contain a summary of interesting research in the field of rapid reading found in various publications. We suggest you read this information carefully and incorporate it into discussions with those who need assurance that it is possible to improve reading speeds and comprehension.

Sections included are:
Grouping
Machines vs. Hand Pacing
Retention of Gains
General Information

You may want to read some of the articles in full to better equip yourself with knowledge of what has been done in the field of reading improvement.

research on the teaching of rapid reading

Grouping

AMBLE, BRUCE R. "Reading by Phrases," *California Journal of Educational Research*, 18 (May 1967), 116–124.

> Summarizes and discusses the implications of three studies relating to phrase reading training for intermediate and junior high school pupils. Concludes that phrase reading training can increase perceptual span and reading comprehension and rate "with students of low, medium, and high reading achievement" with no "significant advantage or change in reading vocabulary."

AMBLE, BRUCE R., and GORDON BUTLER. "Phrase Reading Training and the Reading Achievement of Slow Learners," *Journal of Special Education*, 1 (Winter 1967), 119–126.

> Discusses 54 students involved in "special classes for slow learners," 28 in the phrase training program and 26 in a program involving selected reading exercises. Each group had 15 training sessions over a three-week period. The phrase training group made greater gains in rate.

ROBINSON, F. G. "An Aid for Improving Rate," *Journal of Educational Research*, 27 (February 1934), 434–455.

> College freshmen were trained to read in spaced phrases of slowly increasing length; at end of 10 weeks, "reading rate as measured by four tests had increased 28 percent and comprehension accuracy had shown a small gain (5 percent)." Recommends this type of training as possibly suitable for elementary school pupils.

SUTHERLAND, JEAN. "The Relationship between Perceptual Span and Rate of Reading," *Journal of Educational Psychology*, 37 (September 1946), 373–380.

> Results show that "training calculated to improve perceptual span will also improve rate of reading and rate of perception." Results are "inconclusive" but seem to suggest that "the group that had previous training in perceptual span made faster initial progress in improvement in rate than a comparable group that had not had training in perceptual span."

WALTON, HOWARD N. "Vision and Rapid Reading," *American Journal of Optometry*, 34 (1957), 73–82.

> Gives historical background of eye movement studies and notes

that, at a distance of 16 inches, a person can see 1.1 inches on either side of a fixation point. This means he can see relatively clearly three words of five letters each and "by utilizing general word shape, context and familiar letter groups, a word at either end of the central fixation point (may) be deduced." Notes that average adult reader fixates on each word for $^1/_4$ second, and the saccadic movement is $^3/_{50}$ of a second.

machines vs. hand pacing

BERGER, ALLEN. "Are Machines Needed to Increase Reading Rate?" *Educational Technology*, 9 (August 1969), 59–60.

Discusses findings of research relating to the use of tachisto-scopic and pacing devices and concludes that "at this point in time, when teaching groups of students, what can be done with machines can be done as well, if not better, without." Suggests that these findings may in part reflect the software put into the hardware. Emphasizes that the findings refer to groups of students and urges attention be given "to the two or three students in nearly every classroom" who may profit from the use of individual machines.

BERGER, ALLEN. "Increasing Reading Rate with Paperbacks," *Reading Improvement*, 4 (Fall 1967), 47–53, 57.

Gives specific suggestions on how to increase reading rate with paperbacks. Contains a discussion of fixations, recognition, vocalization, subvocalization, and regressions. Emphasizes the need for students to have an increased understanding of the reading process and the concept of flexibility. Includes a brief listing of paperbacks and two sample quizzes.

KARLIN, ROBERT. "Machines and Reading: A Review of Re-search," *Clearing House*, 32 (1958), 349–352.

Reports on 13 investigations involving machines and reading done during previous two decades. These were grouped at four levels: elementary, secondary, college, and adult. Found that of the 12 studies measuring natural reading against machine read-ing, 11 of "the groups that received training in the former either equaled or surpassed the machine groups in rate of reading." Suggested spending more money on materials rather than on machines.

Retention of Gains (Conclusion: Gains can be retained!)

BERGER, ALLEN. "Effectiveness of Four Methods of Increasing Reading Rate, Comprehension, and Flexibility," in J. Allen Figurel (ed.), *Forging Ahead in Reading*, 1967 Proceedings, Volume 12, Part 1. Newark, Delaware; International Reading Association, 1968, 588–596 (Doctoral dissertation, Syracuse University, 1966).

> Found that all four methods—tachistoscopic, controlled reader, controlled pacing, and paperback scanning (hand pacing)—produced significant (p. 01) gains in rate, the paperback scanning method being significantly superior to the other methods. No significant change appeared in comprehension level. All gains were retained when checked eight weeks after the completion of training.

COSPER, RUSSELL, and NEWELL C. KEPHART. "Retention of Reading Skills," *Journal of Educational Research*, 49 (November 1955), 211–216.

> Describes reading program at Purdue. Study aimed at retention of speed gains; 204 students enrolled in 1950 were pre- and post-tested with Diagnostic Reading Tests, Survey Section; control was 208 students who volunteered. Fourteen months later, invitations for retesting were sent out and 38 in E group and 28 in C group responded. Results: A significant faction (ca. 60 percent) of the speed gained during the developmental program was retained after fourteen months.

RAY, DARREL D. "The Permanency of Gains Made in College Reading Improvement Programs," in J. Allen Figurel (Ed.), Improvement of Reading Through Classroom Practice, 1964 Proceedings 9. Newark, Delaware: International Reading Association, 1964, 192–193.

> Reviews fifteen studies dealing with retention of gain since 1950. Seven indicated a retention of gain in reading rate, while five reported a decline, and three reported additional gain beyond the rate attained on the post-test.

SCHWARTZ, MARVIN F. "An Evaluation of the Effectiveness of the Reading Training Given in the U.S. Naval School, Preflight," USN School Aviation Medicine Research Report, 1957.

> Describes program indicating rate of college level subjects increased while comprehension decreased as a result of training. Retention was checked eight weeks later and it was found that 90 percent of the gain was retained.

STATON, THOMAS F. "Preliminary Evidence on Permanency of Reading Rate Increases Following Intensive Training in a Reading Lab," *American Psychologist*, 5 (1950), 341–342.

Twelve Air Force officers who had completed the standard reading improvement lab course developed and supervised by Air University were located and, after a time lapse ranging from four months to one year, had completed another course similar to the first. Found that 1) a reading course improves rate and comprehension, 2) following end of course there is a drop in reading rate but not to the point of beginning rate, and 3) "repetition of the course tends to result in a reading rate higher than that achieved at the end of the original course."

general

LAFFITTE, RONDEAU G., JR. "Analysis of Increased Rate of Reading of College Students," *Journal of Developmental Reading*, 7 (Spring 1964), 165–174.

Reports on 56 college freshmen divided into three groups. One group received skimming practice exclusively; the second group, rapid reading drill only; the third group, skimming and rapid reading practice. The second and third groups used tachistoscopic and pacing devices. Training lasted two months. All three groups significantly increased reading rate, with most of the gains for the three groups occurring during the first month of training.

MAXWELL, MARTHA J., and ARTHUR C. MUELLER. "Relative Effectiveness of Techniques and Placebo Conditions in Changing Reading Rate," *Journal of Reading*, 11 (December 1967), 191–194.

Involved 120 students at the University of Maryland. Forty were given a handout containing specific suggestions for increasing reading rate, with instructions to practice for a week. A second group of 40 students "were given materials designed to motivate them to read faster by stressing the importance of rapid reading but without a description of specific techniques." The remaining 40 students served as a control group. "The experimental group given techniques and urged to practice showed significantly greater rate gains (33 percent improvement) than either the group receiving motivational material (11 percent improvement) or the controls (9 percent improvement).

the ebbinghaus retention curve

This can also be called the "curve of forgetting." The learning curve shows the loss of information for the passive reader—the person who simply picks up a book and reads.

For the person who is an active reader and who stresses the comprehension building techniques learned in a rapid reading course, the curve is no longer valid. Although there are no statistics to indicate how much more a person retains and over what period of time, it is safe to assume that the active reader will retain more information for at least twice as long as the passive reader.

RETENTION CURVE
(Ebbinghaus, 1885)

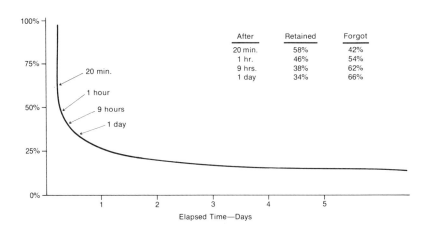

After	Retained	Forgot
20 min.	58%	42%
1 hr.	46%	54%
9 hrs.	38%	62%
1 day	34%	66%

Elapsed Time—Days

how to construct your own comprehension test

You can create your own comprehension test quite easily to test reading comprehension and to make participants aware of their reading habits.

Choose ten consecutive pages of an article, dividing each of the ten pages into three sections. On a separate sheet, make three columns corresponding to the three sections on the pages. For each column, choose words that appeared in the article. Mix these words together for each column, to form three columns of equal length, representing the three sections of the ten pages.

Ask the participants to read the article. Then instruct them to circle the words on your test which they remember as being in the article just read. Almost all students will circle more words in the first column than in the second, and more in the second than in the third.

Most readers do not realize that they start out slowly on each page and then hurry toward the end of the page, and consequently miss more of what is in the last third of the page. This test can make them conscious of this by showing that they remembered more from the first third of each page and their comprehension is lowest on the last third.

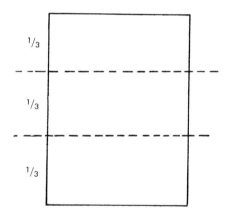
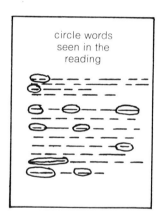

level of difficulty

It is not necessary to tell class members the level of difficulty of the books they use, but you can integrate this information into your instruction in a variety of ways.

Grade level (level of difficulty) is determined through a formula which examines the length and difficulty of words, degree of complication of study, sentence length, etc. Calculating grade level accurately involves a complex and time-consuming procedure. However, here is a simplified formula for determining the approximate level of difficulty which will be close enough for purposes of your rapid reading class.

1. Choose five half-pages which are as representative as possible of the text.
2. In each sentence:
   a. Count 1 for each word of one or two syllables
   b. Count 3 for each word of three or more syllables
   c. Count numbers and proper names as 1
   d. Count each clause of a compound sentence as a sentence.
3. Divide the total count for each sentence by 2. The result is the grade level for the sentence.
4. Add the grade levels for all sentences and divide by the number of sentences. The answer is the grade level for the half-page.
5. Average the grade levels for the five half-pages. The answer is a good estimate of the grade level for the book.
6. If you wish, write the grade levels at the front of the books that class members use in class.

paperbacks and their levels of difficulty

Following is a list of Dell paperbacks, arranged by grade level. You might choose some from each level for practice books in your rapid reading session. This list is provided for your information, but you can inform your class members of the levels of the books they use if you wish.

Grade Level 7–8
Street Rod / Baseball's Unforgettables / The Bells of St. Mary's / The Bridge at Toko-Ri / Cheaper by the Dozen / Great Tales of Horror (Poe) / Jamie

Level 9–10
April Morning / Bridge at Andau / Crash Club / Drums Along the Mohawk / Goodbye, Mr. Chips / High Gear / Hiroshima / Man-Eaters of Kumaon / The Miracle Worker

Level 11–12
A Bell for Adano / Billy Budd / Here to Stay / The
Citadel / The Scarlet Letter / Genghis Khan / Green
Mansions / Farmer in the Sky

Level 13–14
All the King's Men / Anna Karenina / Raise High
the Roof Beam / Crime and Punishment / Fathers
and Sons / Pride and Prejudice / Lord Jim /
Frankenstein / A Day in the Life of Pres. Kennedy /
The Light in the Forest / Lost Cities & Vanished
Civilizations / A Night to Remember / Quality of
Courage / Road Rocket Hot Rod / Flying
Saucers—Serious Business / Our Hearts Were
Young and Gay /

The Pearl / Pebble in the Sky / The Red Pony /
Shane / Tales from the House Behind / The Moon is
Down / The Mouse on the Moon / Huckleberry Finn /
The Member of the Wedding / The Sea of Grass /
Seven Days in May / A Separate Peace / Fifty Great
American Short Stories / King Solomon's Mines /
The President's Plane is Missing / Fail-Safe / The
Kennedy Wit / Quo Vadis / Complete Short Stories
of Mark Twain / Scaramouche / Heart of Darkness /
Catch 22 / Cat's Cradle / The Hound of the
Baskervilles

publicity aids

Following are ideas on publicity that can help you spread the word about your rapid reading class if you are offering a class at a school. This list should start your thinking toward what will work best for your school. If you are teaching for a church, business, or other organization, some of these same ideas slightly modified will work with your non-school group also.

1. Send a letter to parents of new students and to returning students before they come to school in the fall or for a new term. This letter should announce the rapid reading class and give instructions on how to pre-register for the course. (Sample letters follow.) Schools who use this approach tell us that it always helps to get more students into their classes.
2. A new student orientation is a good place to make a personal announcement or presentation about the course. This is highly successful because new students are always looking for ways to assist them in surviving their new year.
3. Set up a rapid reading registration area at your regular course registration preceding each semester or quarter. Then make a personal announcement telling what can be gained from the course.
4. Place announcements in the school newspaper and in the "news and notes" circular for faculty and staff.
5. Make personal announcements wherever students gather on campus—student assemblies and forums, student lounges, meetings, etc.
6. Use mailbox stuffers to announce the program to all students.
7. Give a short "mini-demonstration" of what you consider the high points of the course—free, of course. You might give an initial timed test, teach the Basic Z and allow some practice time, then test again—most students will increase with just this basic instruction. Of course they should not expect to retain their new speed without the benefit of the grouping and pacing instruction and continued practice.
8. Promote with the idea of learning to read and have fun: have fun in the class while you learn, have fun getting your reading done faster, have fun with your extra time!
9. Enlist faculty members to encourage their students to take the course. A few enthusiastic teachers are more valuable than all

the publicity you can do, so demonstrate and explain the course to your faculty friends, and they should be happy to encourage their students to take the course.

10. Tell the experiences of other students at your school who have benefited from the program—or, let the students tell their classmates their positive reactions and the benefits they gained.

11. Contact other local schools (colleges, high schools, etc.) and invite their students to attend your class.

12. Encourage students to invite members of their family and friends to attend with them, especially when classes are held in the evening.

13. Announce that room size is limited (if it really is) and that enrollment will be on a first come, first served basis.

14. If you have residence halls on campus, put up posters, make announcements at dorm meetings. Get the residence hall staff excited about what this can do for students to make better use of their study time.

This list is just a start. Whatever works best for you—that's what you should do! Just be sure to get the word out. Enthusiastically!

Following is a sample letter which can be sent to parents of new students:

Dear Parents,

We look forward to having your son or daughter at our school in a few weeks!

As you are well aware, all students are faced with an enormous amount of required reading. Couple this mountain of reading with inefficiently developed study skills, and many students quickly find themselves falling behind in their work. This inability to keep up with required reading and to efficiently digest what is read is a major cause of student failure. We feel this is a significant problem since few students have had the benefit of training in improved reading and study skills.

To assist our students in overcoming this threat to their success, we have arranged to offer a Rapid Reading Course on campus shortly after school begins. This rapid reading and study skills course is guaranteed to at least double reading speed, but our experience with this program shows that most students triple their speeds with improved comprehension and study skills. This well-planned course lays the groundwork for a successful career.

Since this is a service which (school name) cannot provide in its normal instructional program, an additional fee is necessary. Tuition for this inexpensive three-week course is $_____. This fee will be refunded if your son or daughter does not at least double his reading efficiency.

During regular course registration on (date) there will be an opportunity to pre-register for the reading course. Please encourage your son or daughter to take advantage of this opportunity now.
Cordially,

(from Principal, Counselor, Instructor, etc.)

Following is a sample letter which can be sent to returning students.

Dear Student,

A Rapid Reading Course will be offered at (school) during the coming semester. Through previous programs here and on other campuses, we have found that students benefit greatly from development of reading skills, especially in the improvement of reading speed and comprehension.

This Rapid Reading Program has been scheduled to meet on (day), (dates of three class sessions), from (beginning-ending time). This course requires little study outside of the class sessions and encourages you to practice your new reading skills on your daily assignments.

Since this is a service which (school) cannot provide in its normal instructional program, an additional fee of $_____ is necessary for this three-week course. During regular course registration on (date) there will be an opportunity to pre-register for this course to assure yourself of a place in the class.

Please give serious consideration to the benefits you can gain from this course through improved reading speed and comprehension.

Cordially,

(from Principal, Counselor, Instructor, etc.)

(Sample News Release for Campus Newspaper)

NEW COURSE ON CAMPUS INCREASES READING SPEED

By special arrangement, Professor _____ has been trained to offer a Rapid Reading course on our campus. Since our instructor is teaching the course, it can be offered conveniently on campus, with benefits that usually are missing in speedreading courses.

The best part of this arrangement is the cost—only $_____! And it is guaranteed. Your money is refunded if your beginning reading rate is not at least doubled in 21 days, with normal comprehension.

Last year thousands of students took rapid reading courses, with an average increase of three times the beginning reading rate. Most students go from about 300 words per minute to about 1,000, and many show a remarkable increase even in the first class session.

This Rapid Reading course also teaches study skills such as flexible reading, techniques for really understanding textbook materials, organizing and studying for exams. Wouldn't you like to be able to read that assignment in half the time, while outlining, underlining and really studying at the same time? This course shows you how to make the best use of your study time.

The course is short! A total of six hours is spent in three two-hour sessions over a period of three weeks. In addition, students practice reading exercises for a half hour per day.

Administrators and students alike have praised the effectiveness of this program. Comments such as "It was all that I anticipated—and more" or "This course is one of the very most helpful things I ever took" are typical of the reactions.

The first sessions will begin _____ and will be held at _____. You may pre-register for the course by _____. For further information, please contact _____ at _____.

(Sample Announcements for News Bulletins)

1. Reading efficiency is an indispensable skill for today's student— and you can't beat the price. Thousands of students have already profited from rapid reading, a short, expertly-instructed, inexpensive and fully-guaranteed course in rapid reading and study skills. The course stresses the outstanding facts of today's learning scene: vastly increased reading requirements and diminished

study time. Why not attend the next session and make this skill work for your benefit? If you don't double your beginning reading speed, we'll refund your $_____ tuition fee. Pre-register at _____.

      Class Dates:
      Place:
      Time:

2. Why pay $350, $250, $175 or even $100 for a rapid reading course that lasts six to eight weeks, when the Rapid Reading course taught by _____ is available for only $_____ and takes only six hours of in-class time? Since this Rapid Reading course promises to at least double your reading speed or refunds your money, what have you to lose? Pre-register at _____.

      Class dates:
      Place:
      Time:

3. The Rapid Reading course on campus will revolutionize your study habits! And at only $_____ for the three-week program! This effective, academically oriented and fully guaranteed course in rapid reading and study skills will be taught by _____ and it will require a minimum of class time. It is a must for students interested in gaining maximum advantage from their education. Remember, if the course doesn't at least double your habitual reading speed in 21 days, your entire tuition fee will be refunded. Pre-register at _____.

      Class dates:
      Place:
      Time:

(Sample Announcement for Student Handout)

ANNOUNCING!
RAPID READING COURSE

    A Rapid Reading course will be offered on our campus soon. This is a great opportunity for you to increase your reading speed and efficiency in a short, inexpensive program. Consider the following:

    *Low Cost   —$_____ per person.
    *Minimum Class Time —Three two-hour sessions over a three-week period.

*Academic Emphasis	—Professor ———— from our faculty will teach the course right on campus.
*Simplicity	—No reading machines, gimmicks or complicated aids.
*Guaranteed	—Your full tuition is refunded if your beginning speed is not at least doubled in 21 days with a half hour of practice each day.

PLACE ————————
DATES ————————
TIME ————————

DON'T WAIT! REGISTER NOW AT ——————————————.

sources for principal professional instruments in a reading laboratory

Reading Accelerators

AVR Rateometer—Audio Visual Research, 531 S. Plymouth Court, Chicago, Illinois 60605

Keystone Reading Pacer—Keystone View Company, Meadville, Pennsylvania 16335

Reading Rate Controller—Stereo Optical Company, 3539 N. Kenton, Chicago, Illinois 60641

Shadowscope—Lafayette Instrument Company, 26 N. 26th Street, Lafayette, Indiana 47904

Tachistoscopes

Keystone Tachistoscope (group)—Keystone View Company, Meadville, Pennsylvania 16335

Tachistoscope (individual)—Lafayette Instrument Company, 26 N. 26th Street, Lafayette, Indiana 47904

Renshaw Tachistoscopic Trainer (individual)—Stereo Optical Company, 3539 North Kenton, Chicago, Illinois 60641

Visual Screening and Diagnostic Instruments

Keystone Visual-Survey Telebinocular—Keystone View Company, Meadville, Pennsylvania 16335

The Ortho-Rater (Bausch & Lomb Occupational Vision Test)— Bausch & Lomb Optical Company, Rochester, New York

The Opthalmograph (for photographing eye movements while reading)—American Optical Company, Southbridge, Mass. 01550.

Reading Tests

California Test Bureau, 5916 Hollywood Blvd. Los Angeles, California 90028

Educational Testing Service, 20 Nassau Street, Princeton, N.J. 08540

The Psychological Corporation, 522 5th Avenue, New York, N.Y. 10036

Science Research Associates, 57 W. Grand Avenue, Chicago, Illinois 60610

World Book Company, Yonkers, New York 10705

Reading Films

Harvard Reading Films (college-adult level)—Harvard University Press, Cambridge, Massachusetts 02138

Iowa Reading Training Films (high school level)—Bureau of Audio-Visual Instruction, Extension Division, State University of Iowa, Iowa City, Iowa 52240

appendices

appendix a

The following pages illustrate recommended content for the overhead projection transparencies necessary in teaching a course in natural rapid reading as described in this book. The illustrations are of the actual transparencies used in teaching the highly success- ful AGP Rapid Reading course. As you anticipate teaching your own course in rapid reading based on the suggestions given in this book, you will want to make certain that your transparencies have essentially the same content as the transparencies illustrated on the following pages. AGP Incorporated and the author of this book have released the right to you to duplicate the transparencies illustrated here. If you feel that making your own transparencies is inconven- ient, you may contact the publisher of this book for assistance in obtaining ready-made overhead projection transparencies. The ad- dress is given below:

Quill Publications
Libertyville, Illinois
60048

WELCOME TO

ACHIEVING **GREATER POTENTIAL**

RAPID READING COURSE

©**AGP Inc.**

A G P READING REGISTRATION CARD

Name _____ Age _____ Years of Education _____
(Beyond Kindergarten)

Group _____ Instructor _____

1. _____ 2. _____ 3. _____

	Course Record—Words Per Minute			
Session	Opening	Middle	End	Comprehension
1				
2				
3				

Minnesota Speed of Reading Test

Pre-Test   Post-Test
(Form A)   (Form B)

Correct _____ Correct _____

Rate _____ Rate _____

How to figure:
1. Determine the number of correct paragraphs. Put that in "correct" above.
2. Multiply that "correct" number by 50.
3. Divide that result by the number of minutes read (either 6 or 3). Put that number in "rate" above.

How to figure:
1. Find the number of whole pages read and multiply by the words per page (WPP) figure for your book.
2. Add up the lines on the partial pages read and multiply by the words per line (WPL) figure for your book.
3. Add the WPP and WPL totals to get total words read.
4. Divide this total by the number of minutes read to get words per minute (WPM).

©**AGP Inc.**

Not "Speedreading" -

but...

an increased "range of speed"

is our goal.

Rapid Reading roots are in
GOOD STUDY HABITS...

If speed is up

    then concentration should be up.

    then comprehension should be up,

    then retention should be up,

Each Step Leads to the Next!

3 TYPES OF READING MATERIAL

Light	MEDIUM	**HEAVY**
* novels	* newspapers	* textbooks
* short stories	* magazines	* journals
* plays	* personal development	* class notes

Your speed in HEAVY reading will improve in proportion to your improvement in LIGHT reading -

For example: if you double in LIGHT reading from 250 to 500 words per minute you should also double in HEAVY reading from 125 to 250 wpm.

©AGP Inc.

3 KINDS OF READERS

Motor reader poor	Lip mover, vocalizer, says words aloud or to himself.
Auditory reader average	Word thinker, hears a page of print though his organs of speech are at rest.
Visual reader rapid	From the page to perception - nothing said, nothing heard, everything seen.

©AGP Inc.

READING RATES

Limits

Vocalizer	— Motor Reader	— 150 wpm
Subvocalizer	— Word Thinker	— 300 wpm
Visual Reader	— Direct Perception	— 800+

Averages

Types of reading material	words per minute
Light—narrative	250-350
Medium—mix of narrative and factual	200-225
Heavy—no narrative—all details and facts	100-150

In our education system, reading instruction stops at grade eight. Further gains in reading skills are on an individual basis.

©AGP Inc.

REGRESSIONS & FIXATIONS

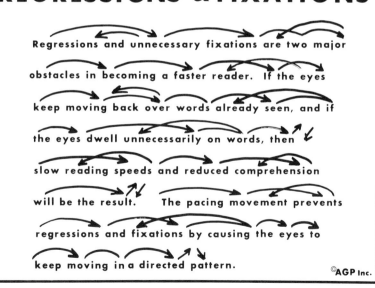

Regressions and unnecessary fixations are two major obstacles in becoming a faster reader. If the eyes keep moving back over words already seen, and if the eyes dwell unnecessarily on words, then slow reading speeds and reduced comprehension will be the result. The pacing movement prevents regressions and fixations by causing the eyes to keep moving in a directed pattern.

©AGP Inc.

TWO MAJOR PROBLEMS

Regression

PACING

1. Eyes follow motion – create that motion

2. Forcing the eyes in a directed pattern
   (a) across the line
   (b) down the page

Fixations

(stops too often)
stops too long)

GROUPING

1. Eyes must stop to see

2. Making the eyes see more than 5 or 6 symbols at a stop = fewer stops

3. Increased speed and span of perception is the key.

©AGP Inc.

©AGP Inc.

*Ygud ud s dorvusk yio drvtry vifr eguvg nyst biy nr
ntijrb, Ug tiy gubf yrg jrt yi ybfrtdysbfubh uym troity
sy ibvr yi tiyt brstrdy GNU grsfwystyrtd,{

Kiij sy rsvg kubr ub yrtnd ig y yne satun durectkt au
wirdob seb. Kiij at eacg krub ub trerns if tge batyrak
griyos if wirds ub tge sebtebce, Nive tiyr etes frin orgase
ti ograse ubstead if stioobung ib eacg wird, Ti ebabke tiy
ti see akk tge wirds ub a ograsem kiij Sey yo ab ete nivenebt
rgttgn as tiy nive frin ograse ti ograse, oractucubg gicoubg
tiyr etes ti estabkusg rgttgnucak nivenebt scriss tge oage,
unoatuebtkt oysgubg tiyrseft ti reacg gugg sceedsl.

Ub a few dats tiy wukk resykt ub readubg fatugye abd
skiwer cincregebsuib. Feek tgat tiy are readubg hyst a kuttle
fastwe rsvh yunr ygsy tiy trsf, Yhr isvrt sgiyke ibkt
skuggrjt orecede tiyr etes, tgiygg bit far. Tge tebdcbct ti
regress, uf tiy kise a wird ir ograse. Us gyreatm, byt fuggt
ut. Jeeo nivubg agead.

Tge drukks are desugbed ti extabkusg a batyrak gabut if
raoud readubg. Sey asude a soecufuc tune eacg day ti di tge
drukks. Tgurtt nubytes a dat. Oractuce tiyr bew skukks ub
cinubf weekjs. Cibufdebce cines wutg yse. Yse tiyr bew a
skukks ib akk ttoes if readubg. Gersibakuse tiyr sjukks ti
fut tiyr readubg beeds, Exoerunobt wutg wats ti oerfect tiyr
a sjukks. Duvude sebtebces ubti griyos if wirds, cucckeug
tiyr sjukks. Reud aud reread tge griyos if words as raoudkt
as oissubke. Tge crucke sgiyke firn a varcet fir tiyr etes,
bit tyr wirds wutgub tge curckes, exceot ibce up a wguko.

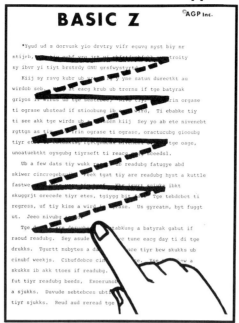

RAPID READING RULES

Don't Push
IMPATIENTLY PUSHING YOURSELF TO REACH HIGH SPEEDS IN A FEW DAYS WILL RESULT IN READING FATIGUE AND SLOWER COMPREHENSION.

Feel Faster
FEEL THAT YOU ARE READING JUST A LITTLE FASTER EACH TIME THAT YOU READ. THE PACER SHOULD ONLY SLIGHTLY PRECEDE YOUR EYES.

Keep Moving
THE TENDENCY TO REGRESS, IF YOU LOSE A WORD OR PHRASE IS GREAT, BUT FIGHT IT. KEEP MOVING AHEAD.

Be Habitual
THE DRILLS ARE DESIGNED TO ESTABLISH A NATURAL HABIT OF RAPID READING. SET ASIDE A SPECIFIC TIME EACH DAY TO DO THE DRILLS. 30 MINUTES A DAY IS THE MINIMUM.

Obey these rules and the results will be an accelerated, natural, good comprehension rate of reading

©AGP Inc.

ACCELERATION
HELPS

INDENT

RAPID RETURN

BOOK HOLDING

 PAGE TURNING

©AGP Inc.

YOU DON'T WRITE WORD BY WORD; YOU WRITE IN PHRASES- READ THAT WAY!

READING THE ABOVE SENTENCE IN PHRASES ONLY REQUIRES FIVE STEPS - NOT THIRTEEN

GROUPING IS A KEY TO COMPREHENSION

©AGP Inc.

GROUPING DRILL CIRCLING

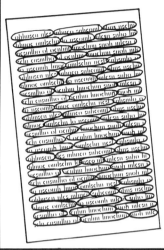

Divide sentences into groups
of words. Circle the groups.
Read and reread the grouped
words as rapidly as possible.
Each circle should form a
target for your eyes, not
the words within the circle.

©AGP Inc.

PACING MOVEMENTS

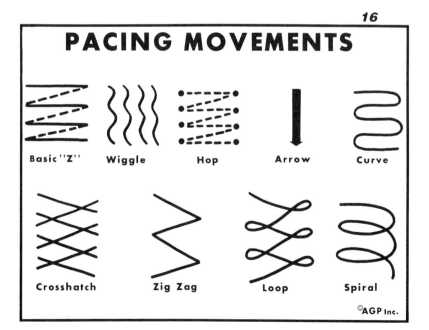

| Basic "Z" | Wiggle | Hop | Arrow | Curve |

| Crosshatch | Zig Zag | Loop | Spiral |

©AGP Inc.

WIGGLE

©AGP Inc.

* Yuud u s dorvu yio drvtr vifr egu nyst biy nr
ntijrb, Ug iy gubf jrt yi rtdysbfu uym troity
sy ibvr yi t brstrdy U grsfwy rtd,(

Kiij sy rsv kubr ub nd ig y e satun rectkt au
wirdob seb. ij at ea krub ub erns if e batyrak
griyos if w ds ub tge ebtebce, ive tiyr tes frin orgase
ti ograse stead if ioobung eacg wir Ti ebabke tiy
ti see akk ge wirds b a ograse kiij S yo ab ete nivenebt
rgttgn as nive fr ograse ograse, actucubg giooubg
tiyr etes ti abkusg tgnucak ivenebt riss tge oage,
unoatuebtkt oys g tiyrs ti rea g gugg sc ds1.

Ub a few dats iy wukk sykt ub adubg f ugye abd
skiwer cincregebs b. Fee gat tiy re read g hyst a kuttle
fastwe rsvh yunr gsy tiy sf, Yh isvrt s yke ibkt
skuggrjt oreced tiyr ete tgiyge it far. Tge tebdcbct ti
regress, uf ti r se. U yreatm, byt fuggt
ut. Jeeo ni

Tge druk yrak gabut if
raoud readu day ti di tge
drukks. Tg ew skukks ub
cinubf week tiyr bew a
skukks ib a r sjukks ti
fut ti oerfect tiyr
a sjuk ce cucckeug
tiyr e as raoudkt

PACING DRILL I

**FAST
FAST
FAST**

1. Read page 1 as fast as possible.
   (Don't worry about comprehension.)

2. Re-read page 1 rapidly and go to
   page 2, still reading rapidly.

3. Repeat pages 1 and 2
   and add page 3, etc.

Don't worry about comprehension
for the moment.

©AGP Inc.

SUMMARY OF
FIRST SESSION

✱ **TYPES OF READING:**　　Light　　Medium　　Heavy

✱ **TYPICAL KINDS OF READERS AND**
　　READING PROBLEMS:　　Motor　　Auditory　　Visual

✱ **REGRESSION AND FIXATION**
　　THE EYES FOLLOW MOTION　　Basic Z　　"wiggle"

✱ **RAPID READING RULES:**　　Don't push

　　　　　　Keep moving　　　　　Feel faster

　　　　　　　　Be habitual

✱ **GROUPING DRILL**　– Circles

✱ **PACING DRILL**　– Fast – Fast – Fast

USE YOUR NEW SKILLS

WE LEARN BY DOING

THE BEST WAY
TO ATTAIN
READING SKILL
IS TO READ.

| 30 MINUTES A DAY |

WE UNLEARN BY NOT DOING

THE BEST WAY
TO BREAK
POOR READING HABITS
IS TO
FORM NEW HABITS.

| USE YOUR NEW SKILLS |

SUMMARY OF
SECOND SESSION

* Fixation Card

* Grouping Drill: slashing phrases

* Pacing Motions: HOP ARROW CURVE

* Comprehension Building I:
  Questioning mind and previewing

* Vocalizing and its cures

* Pacing Drill – 3x3

* Comprehension Building II:
  Previewing exercise

©AGP Inc.

KEYS TO PHRASE READING

GROUP WORDS LOOK AT EACH LINE/IN TERMS OF/THE NATURAL GROUPS OF WORDS/IN THE SENTENCE./MOVE YOUR EYES/ FROM PHRASE TO PHRASE/INSTEAD OF STOPPING/ON EACH WORD.

SOFT FOCUS TO ENABLE YOU TO SEE ALL THE WORDS IN A PHRASE AT ONCE, LOOK SLIGHTLY ABOVE THE PHRASE INSTEAD OF DIRECTLY AT THE LINE OF WORDS.

RHYTHM READ SET UP AN EYE MOVEMENT RHYTHM AS YOU MOVE FROM PHRASE TO PHRASE. PRACTICE "HOPPING" YOUR EYES TO ESTABLISH RHYTHMICAL MOVEMENT ACROSS THE PAGE.

©AGP Inc.

GROUPING DRILL II:
SLASHING

Having mastered circling of groups, now use only a single diagonal line between phrases.

Read and re-read using soft focus.

©AGP Inc.

HOP

©AGP Inc.

*Ygud ud s dorvusk yio drvtry vifr eguvg nyst biy nr ntijrb, Ug tiy qubf yrg irt yi yhfrtdysbfubh uym troity sy ibvr yi tiyt brstrdy GNU grsfwystyrtd,(

Kiij sy rsvg kubr ub yrtnd ig y the brun durectkt au wirdob seb. Kiij at the akub ub trerns if tge batyrak griyos if the tiy tge sehtebce, Nive tiyr etes frin orgase ti ograse ubstead if stioobung ib eacg wird, Ti ebabke tiy ti see akk tge wirds ub a ograsem at a tey yo ab ete nivenebt rgttgn as tiy nive fr ograse ti ograse, oractucubg giooubg tiyr etes a habkusg rgttqnucak nivenebt scriss tge oage, unoatuebtkt oysgubg tiyrseft ti reacg gugg se 1.

Ub a few dats tiy wukk resvkt adubg fatugye abd skiwer cincregebs ek tgat tiy are readubg hyst a kuttle fastwe r h tiy yrey tiy tref. Yhr isvrt sgiyke ihkt skuggrjt orecede tiyr etes, tgiygg bit far. ebdcbct ti regress, uf tiy kise a wird ir ogra gyreatm, byt fuggt ut. Jeeo nivubg agead.

Tge drukks are desugbed ti ex a batyrak gabut if raoud readubg. Sey asude a so ne eacg day ti di tge drukks. Tgurtt nubytes a dat ce tiyr bew skukks ub cinubf weekjs. Cibufdeh yse. Yse tiyr bew a skukks ib akk ttoes i kuse tiyr sjukks ti fut tiyr readubg rs ti oerfect tiyr a sjukks. Duvude rds, cucckeug tiyr sjukks. R rds as raoudkt

COMPREHENSION BUILDER I

A QUESTIONING MIND

1. ACTIVE vs. PASSIVE approach

2. QUESTIONS in the why, what, who, when, how, where areas

Kipling - "I had six honest serving men.
They taught me all I know.
Their names are -
where and what and when and why,
and how and who."

3. ARGUING with author keeps concentration up

©AGP Inc.

COMPREHENSION BUILDER II
PREVIEWING

Using a pacer, look over

1. Covers, inside and out

2. Table of contents

3. Introduction or preface

4. Diagrams, charts, maps

©AGP Inc.

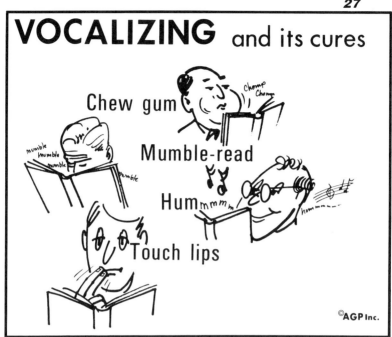

VOCALIZING and its cures

Chew gum

Mumble-read

Hum

Touch lips

©AGP Inc.

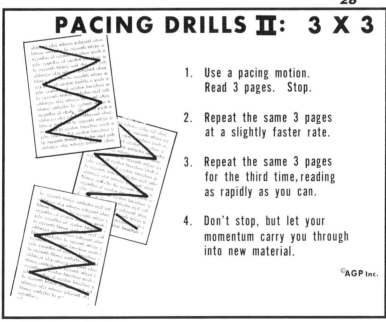

PACING DRILLS II: 3 X 3

1. Use a pacing motion. Read 3 pages. Stop.

2. Repeat the same 3 pages at a slightly faster rate.

3. Repeat the same 3 pages for the third time, reading as rapidly as you can.

4. Don't stop, but let your momentum carry you through into new material.

©AGP Inc.

ARROW

*Ygud ud s dorvusk yio rvtry vifr eguvg nyst biy nr
ntijrb, Ug tiy gubf yrg t yi ybfrtdysbfubh uym troity
sy ibvr yi tiyt brstrdy G grsfwystyrtd,(

Kiij sy rsvg kubr ub y nd ig y yne satun durectkt au
wirdob seb. Kiij at eacg rub ub trerns if tge batyrak
griyos if wirds ub tge seb bce, Nive tiyr etes frin orgase
ti ograse ubstead if stioc ng ib eacg wird, Ti ebabke tiy
ti see akk tge wirds ub a rasem kiij Sey yo ab ete nivenebt
rgttgn as tiy nive frin og se ti ograse, oractucubg giooubg
tiyr etes ti estabkusg rgt nucak nivenebt scriss tge oage,
unoatuebtkt oysgubg tiyrse ti reacg gugg sceedsl.

Ub a few dats t wukk sykt readubg fatugye abd
skiwer cincregebsuib. Peek gat iy are readubg hyst a kuttle
fastwe rsvh yunr ygsy e it f Yhr isvrt sgiyke ibkt
skuggrjt orecede tiyr ete ygg bit far. Tge tebdcbct ti
regress, uf tiy kise a wird r ograse. Us gyreatm, byt fuggt
ut. Jeeo nivubg

Tge drukks batyrak gabut if
raoud readubg. cg day ti di tge
drukks. Tgurt bew skukks ub
cinubf weekjs. e tiyr bew a
skukks ib akk ea yr sjukks ti
fut tiyr readul E} i oerfect tiyr
a sjukks. es , cucckeug
tiyr sjukk re as raoudkt

PREVIEW EXERCISE

1. Using The Arrow Pacing Pattern, skim the entire book in 5 minutes.

2. Read from the beginning for comprehension.

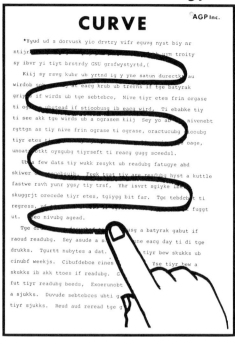

SUMMARY OF THIRD SESSION

❋ GROUPER CARD

❋ PACING COMFORT MOTIONS

CROSSHATCH   ZIG ZAG   LOOP   SPIRAL

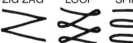

❋ PACING DRILL III: Many fast – Few slow

❋ SKIMMING & SCANNING

❋ COMPREHENSION BUILDING III
Note-taking   Postviewing

❋ FINAL TESTS – LIGHT and HEAVY

©AGP Inc.

GROUPING DRILL III

...ye iy dewtry vifr eguvg nyst biy nr
ntijrb, Ug tiy gu... ...troi...
sy ibvr yi tiyt brstrdy GNU grsfwystyrtd,(

   Kiij sy rsvg kubr ub yrtnd ig y yne satun durectkt au
wirdob seb. Kiij at eacg krub ub trerns if tge batyrak
griyos if wirds ub tge sebtebce, Nive tiyr etes frin orgase
ti ograse u... ...bt
ti see akk ...
rgttgn as t...
tiyr etes t...
unoatuebtkt ...

   Ub a few ... ...le
skiwer cinc...
fastwe rsvh...
skuggrjt or...
regress, uf...
ut. Jeeo nivubg agead.

   Tge drukks are desugbed ti extabkusg a batyrak gabut if
raoud readubg. Sey asude a soecufuc tune eacg day ti di tge
drukks. Tgurtt nubytes a dat. Oractuce tiyr bew skukks ub
cinubf weekjs. Cibufdebce cines wutg yse. Yse tiyr bew a
skukks ib akk ttoes if readubg. Gersibakuse tiyr sjukks ti
fut tiyr readubg beeds, Exoerunobt wutg wats ti oerfect tiyr

AGP Inc.   -4ukks. Duvude sebtebces ubti griyos if wirds, cucckeug
    reread tge griyos if words as raoudkt
     varcet fir tiyr etes,

AGP GROUPER

| | | | | | | | | | | |

ti ograse

1 Cut out center rectangle.
2 Guide grouper down center of page
3 As eyes become accustomed to seeing all the words, extend
  the opening

| | | | | | | | | | | |

1 Cut out end rectangles.
2 As you guide grouper down page, swing eyes from phrase to
  phrase
3 Increase the size of the openings as you are able

CROSSHATCH
AGP Inc.

*Yyud ud s aorvusk yio drvtry vifr eguvg nyst biy nr
ntijrb, ...iy gubf yrg jrt yi ybfrtdysbfubh uym troity
sy ibvr yi tiyt brst... GNU grsfwystyrtd,(

   Kiij sy rsvg kubr ub yrtnd i... satu... ...kt au
wirdob seb. Kiij at eacg kru... crerns if tge...
griyos if wirds ub t... sebtebce, Nive tiyr etes frin orgase
ti ogra... ...d if stioobung ib eacg wird, Ti ebabke tiy
ti se... akk tge wir... ...ograsem kiij Sey yo ab ete nivenebt
rgttgn as tiy nive frin ograse ...ase, oractucu... iiooubg
tiyr etes ti estabkusg rgttgnucak niveneh... tge oage,
unoatuebtkt oysgubg tiyrseft t... ...cy gugg sceedsl.

   U... few dats ...kk resykt ub readubg fatugye abd
skiwer ...egu... ...eek tgat tiy are readubg hyst a kuttle
fastwe rsvh yunr ygsy tiy trsf, ...gjiyke i...
skuggrjt orecede tiyr etes, tgiygg bit far. ...t ti
regress, uf tiy kise a wird ir ogras... ...s gyreatm, byt fuggt
ut. Jeeo nivubg agead.

   Tge ...d ti extabkusg a batyrak gabut if
raoud rea...y. Sey asude a soecufu... ...r ti di tge
drukks. Tgurtt nubytes a dat. Oractuce ... skukks ub
cinubf weekjs. Cibufdebce cines wutg y... ...iyr bew a
skukks ib akk ttoes if readubg. Gersi... ...r sjukks ti
fut tiyr readubg beeds, Exoerunobt ... ci oerfect tiyr
a sjukks. Duvude sebtebces ub... ...rds, cucckeug
tiyr sjukks. Reud aud rere... ...'s as raoudkt

ZIG ZAG

©AGP Inc.

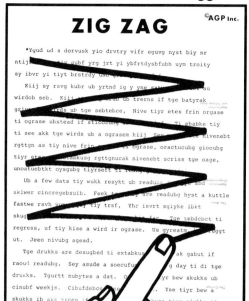

PACING DRILL III

MANY FAST - FEW SLOW

1. Read 25 pages very rapidly.

2. Repeat the first few pages (1-5) reading for comprehension.

3. Begin reading very rapidly (6-30) again, adding a few pages.

4. Repeat a few pages again (6-10), reading for comprehension.

5. Continue, repeating the above steps.

©AGP Inc.

SKIMMING & SCANNING

SKIMMING

- used in NEW material for main ideas
- read only TOPIC sentences

SCANNING

- used in material already read
- know what you seek and find it with a zig-zag pacer

©AGP Inc.

38

LOOP

©AGP Inc.

*Yyud ud s dorvusk yio drvtry vifr eguvg nyst biy nr
ntijrb. Ug tiy gubf yrg jrt yi ybfrtdysbfubh uym troity
sy ibvr yt iyt brstrdy GNU grsfwys td,(

Kiij sy rsvg br ub yrtnd y yne satun du tkt au
wirdob seb. Kiij at eacg ub ub trerns if tge batyrak
griyos if wirds ub tge ebtebce, Nive tiyr etes frin orgase
ti ograse ubstead i stioobung ib eacg wird, Ti ebabke tiy
ti se akk tge ub a ograsem kiij Sey yo ab ete nivenebt
rgtt as y nive frin og e ti ograse ractucu g giooubg
tiyr etes ti estabkusg rgttgnvcak eriss tge oage,
unoatuebtkt oysgubg tiyrseft t eacg gugg sceedsl.

Ub a few dats tiy wukk sykt ub readubg fatugye abd
skiwe cincre ub Feek tgat tiy are readubg hyst a kuttle
fastw uhr ygsy rsf, Yhr isu sgiyke kt
skuggrjt orecede tiyr etes, tgiy e tebdcbct ti
regress, uf tiy kise a wird r ograse. Us gyreatm, byt fuggt
ut. Jeeo nivubg agead

Tge drukks are d ti extabkusg a batyrak gabut if
raoud readubg. S soecufuc tune eacg day ti di tge
drukks. Tgurtt nuby Oractuce tiyr bew skukks ub
cinubf weekjs. Cibufo bew a
skukks ib akk ttoes if r s ti
fut tiyr readubg beeds, Ex tiyr
a sjukks. Duvude sebteb
tiyr sjukks. Reud aud rer

125

SPIRAL

©AGP Inc.

*Ygud ud s dorvusk yio drvtry vifr eguvg nyst biy nr
ntijr... ...fubh uym troity
sy ibvr yi tiyt brstrdy GNU grsfwystyrtd,(

Kiij sy rsvg kubr ub yrtnd ig y yne satun durect... au
wirdob... . Kiij at eacg krub... ...ns if tge baty...ak
gri...s if wirds ub tge sebtebce, Nive tiy...tes f...n orgase
ti og...se ubstead if stioobung ib eacg wird... ...babke tiy
ti see akk tge wirds ub a ograsem kiij Sey yo ab...te nivenebt
rgttgn as tiy nive frin ograse ti ograse, oractucub...giooubg
tiyr... ...ti estabkusg rgttgnu... ...ebt scriss...ge oage,
une...tuebtkt oysgubg tiyrseft ti reacg gugg...ds...

...a few dats tiy wukk resykt ub readubg f...dg...abd
skiwer cinc... ...Each... ...readubg hy...t a kuttle
fastwe rsvh yunr ygsy tiy trsf, Yhr isvrt sgiyke i...t
skug... ...recede tiyr etes, ...it far. Tge te...dcbct ti
r...ress, uf tiy kise a wird ir ograse. Us gy...a...,byt fuggt
ut. ...Jeeo nivubg agead.

Tge drukks... ...ktubkusg a batyrak...abut if
raoud readubg. Sey asude a soecufuc tune eacg...y ti di tge
drukks. Tgurtt nubytes... ...tiyr bew skukks ub
cinubf weekjs. Cibufd... ...s wutg yse. Yse tiyr bew a
skukks ib akk ttoes if... ...Gersibakuse tiyr sjukks ti
fut tiyr readubg beeds, ...wutg wats ti oerfect tiyr
a sjukks. Duvude sebtebces... ...cuckeug
tiyr sjukks. Reud aud rerea... ...dkt

COMPREHENSION BUILDER III

NOTE-TAKING:

Dotting the margin vs. underlining

POSTVIEWING:

Reviewing and underlining the dotted portions

©AGP Inc.

THIS COURSE IS NOT OVER!

The Benefits Are Still To Come.

You have the SKILL –

   now make it a HABIT!

HOW?

   By using your new ... DAILY ...

   on all types of

ACHIEVING
GREATER
POTENTIAL ©AGP Inc.

appendix b

Bibliography

The following lists of books are designed to assist you in expanding your knowledge of the field of reading improvement and of reading problems and their correction. The list is divided into two priorities:

Priority 1: A list of paperback books which blend speed reading and study skills. They provide illustrations, techniques and applications of speed reading to the academic world, and are therefore valuable for both teacher and students. These books should have top priority as you recommend materials to participants for further study on their own.

Priority 2: A list of books available in the area of reading improvement which ought to be available in every college library.

Priority 1

1. Carroll, David. *Instant Speed Reading.* (New York: Universal Publishing & Distributing Company, 1970, Paper, 75¢.)
2. Herrick, Myron Q. *Reading for Speed and Better Grades.* (New York: Dell Publishing Co., Inc. 1963, Paper, $1.25.)
3. Johnson, Ben E. *Learn to Rapid-Read.* (Indianapolis: Howard W. Sams & Co., Inc. 1973, Paper, $4.50.)
4. Johnson, Ben E. *Rapid Reading With A Purpose.* (Glendale: Regal Books Division, G/L Publications, 1973, Paper, $3.25.)

5. Leedy, Paul D. *Improve Your Reading: A Guide to Greater Speed, Understanding and Enjoyment.* (New York: McGraw-Hill Book Company, Inc., 1956. Paper, $2.85.)
6. Maberly, Norman C. *Mastering Speed Reading.* (New York: New American Library, 1966. Paper, 60¢.)
7. Schiavone, James. *You Can Read Faster.* (New York: Grosset & Dunlap, 1969. Paper, $1.25.)
8. Spargo, Edward. *The Now Student: Freshman Reading and Study Skills.* (Providence: Jamestown Publishers, Inc., 1971. Paper, $3.95.)
9. Spargo, Edward, Editor. *Selections from the Black.* (Providence: Jamestown Publishers, Inc., 1970. Paper. Series of 3 books.)
10. Waldman, John. *Rapid Reading Made Simple.* (New York: Doubleday & Company, Inc. 1958, $1.95.)

Priority 2

Betts, Emmett A., *Foundations of Reading Instruction* (New York, American Book Company, 1946).

Bond, Guy L., and Bond, Eva, *Developmental Reading in High School* (New York, The Macmillan Company, 1942).

Center, Stella S., and Persons, Gladys L., *Experiences in Reading and Thinking* (New York, The Macmillan Company, 1948).

Chicago University, *Clinical Studies in Reading,* I and II (Chicago, University of Chicago Press, I-1949; II-1953).

Dolch, Edward William, *Problems in Reading* (Champaign, Ill., The Garrard Press, 1948).

Durrell, Donald D., *Improvement of Basic Reading Abilities* (New York, World Book Company, 1940).

———, and Sullican, Helen B., *High Interest-Low Vocabulary Booklist* (Boston, Boston Univ., School of Education, 1950).

Ephron, Beulah Kanter, *Emotional Difficulties in Reading* (New York, Julian Press, Inc., 1953).

Gates, Arthur I., *Improvement of Reading,* A Program of Diagnostic and Remedial Methods (New York, The Macmillan Company, 1974).

Gray, William S., ed., *Classroom Techniques in Improving Reading,* Supplementary Educational Monographs, No. 69 (Chicago, University of Chicago Press, October, 1949).

———, *Improving Reading in All Curriculum Areas,* Supplementary Educational Monographs, No. 76 (Chicago, University of Chicago Press, 1952).

————, *Keeping Reading Programs Abreast of the Times*, Supplementary Educational Monographs, No. 72 (Chicago, University of Chicago Press, 1950).

————, *Promoting Growth Toward Maturity in Interpreting What is Read*, Supplementary Educational Monographs, No. 74 (Chicago, University of Chicago Press, 1951).

————, *Promoting Personal and Social Development Through Reading*, Supplementary Educational Monographs, No. 64 (Chicago, University of Chicago Press, October, 1947).

————, *Reading in an Age of Mass Communication*, Report of the Committee on Reading at the Secondary School and College Levels of the National Council of Teachers of English (New York, Appleton-Century-Crofts, Inc., 1949).

————, *Reading in the Content Fields*, Supplementary Educational Monographs, No. 62 (Chicago, University of Chicago Press, 1947).

Harris, Albert J., *How to Increase Reading Ability* (New York, Longmans, Green & Company, 1948).

Havighurst, Robert J., "Characteristics, Interests, and Needs of Pupils That Aid in Defining the Nature and Scope of the Reading Program," in W.S. Gray, ed., *Adjusting Reading Programs to Individuals*, Supplementary Educational Monograph, No. 52 (Chicago, University of Chicago Press, October, 1941), pp. 53–59.

Jennings, Frank G., "That Johnny May Read," *Saturday Review*, Vol. XXXIX, No. 5 (February 4, 1956), pp. 7–9, 39–41.

LaBrant, Lou, *An Evaluation of the Free Reading in Grades 10, 11 and 12 for the Class of 1935*, Ohio State University Studies: Contributions in Education No. 2, rev. ed. (Columbus, Ohio State University Press, 1936).

————, *We Teach English* (New York, Harcourt, Brace & Company, Inc., 1951), pp. 52–60, 225–263.

Loban, Walter, *High Interest—Low Vocabulary Booklist*, B1158, Contra Costa County Schools (Martinez, California, 1951).

McKillop, Anne Selley, *The Relationship Between the Reader's Attitude and Certain Types of Reading Response* (New York, Bureau of Publications, Teachers College, Columbia University, 1952).

Morse, William C., Ballantine, Francis A., and Dixon, Robert W., *Studies in the Psychology of Reading* (Ann Arbor, University of Michigan Press, 1951).

National Council of Teachers of English, Commission on the English Curriculum, The English Language Arts, NCTE Curriculum Series, Vol. I (New York, Appleton-Century-Crofts, Inc., 1952), pp. 397–413.

National Society for the Study of Education, *Reading in the High School and College*, Forty-seventh Yearbook, Part II, (Chicago, University of Chicago Press, 1948).

Pittsburgh University, *Report of the Sixth Annual Conference on Reading* (Pittsburgh, University of Pittsburgh Press, 1950).

Robinson, Helen M., Ed., *Promoting Maximal Reading Growth Among Able Learners*, Supplementary Educational Monographs No. 81 (Chicago, University of Chicago Press, December, 1954).

———, *Why Pupils Fail in Reading* (Chicago, University of Chicago Press, 1946).

Strang, Ruth M., Gilbert, Christine B., and Scoggin, Margaret C., *Gateways to Readable Books: an Annotated Graded List of Books in Many Fields for Adolescents Who Find Reading Difficult*, 2nd ed. (New York, H.W. Wilson Company, 1952).

Strang, Ruth, McCullough, Constance M., and Traxler, Arthur E., *Problems in the Improvement of Reading*, 2nd ed. (New York, McGraw-Hill Book Company, 1955).

Witty, Paul, *How To Become a Better Reader* (Chicago, Science Research Associates, Inc., 1953).

appendix c

In each case the name of the test is indicated with the year it was prepared. The grade levels that the test is appropriate for are indicated along with the number of minutes necessary for students to complete the tests. We have also indicated what general areas of reading comprehension the tests cover. In each case the name of the author or publisher is indicated so that you may be able to order tests directly from them. Each of the tests indicated will vary in quality and difficulty. With one exception, no recommendations are given for specific tests to be used in your rapid reading course. The Minnesota Speed of Reading Test is recommended because it is brief, requiring only six minutes of class time to administer.

Test	Grade	Sub-Tests	No. Forms	Min.	Author-Publisher
Am'n School Achievement Tests (R1958)	7–9	Sentence, word meaning; paragraph meaning	4	40	Pratt, Young & Crockerville; Bobbs-Merrill
American School Reading Tests (1955)	10–13	Vocabulary; reading rate; comprehension	2	80	Pratt & Love; Bobbs-Merrill
Buffalo Reading Test for Speed & Comprehension (R1965)	9–16	Speed; comprehension	2	35	Wagner; Foster & Stewart Publishing Corp.
Burnett Reading Series: Survey Test					Burnett; Scholastic Testing Svc.
Advanced (1967)	7–9	Vocabulary; rate and accuracy; comprehension	1	38	
Senior (1968)	10–12		1		
California Phonics Survey (R1963)	7–16	Vowel-consonant confusion, reversals, rigidity, etc.	2	40	Brown & Cottrell; California Test Bureau
California Reading Test		Vocabulary, comprehension			Tiegs & Clark; California Test Bureau
Jr. High (R1963)	7–9		4	80	
Advanced (R1963)	9–14		3	80	
California Study Methods Survey (R1958)	7–13	Attitudes toward school; mechanics of study; planning and system; verification	1	35–50	Carter; California Test Bureau
California Survey Series: Survey of Reading Achievement					Tiegs & Clark; California Test Bureau
Jr. High (1959)	7–9		2	45	
Advanced	9–12		2	45	
Commerce Reading Comprehension (R1958)	12–16+		1	65	Dept. of Psychological Testing; DePaul Univ.

Test	Grades	Areas Measured	No.	Time	Author; Publisher
Coop. English Tests: Reading Comprehension (R1960)	9–14	Vocabulary; level of comprehension; speed of comprehension	3	45	Derrick, Harris & Walker; Test Div., Educational Testing Service
Coop. Inter-Am'n Tests-Reading (1950)	1–13	Vocabulary; comprehension (level and speed)	4		Comm. on Modern Languages of Am'n Council on Ed'n; Coop. Test Div., Educational Testing Service
Cumulative Reading Record (R1956)	9–12		1		Skinner; National Council of Teachers of English
Davis Reading Test Series I (R1962) Series II (1962)	11–13 8–11	Level of Comp., speed of comprehension	4 4	40 40	Davis & Davis; Psychological Corp.
Diagnostic Reading Tests Upper Level (R1963)	7–13	Survey; vocabulary; comprehension; rate of reading; word attack	2		F. Triggs; Committee on Diagnostic Reading Tests
Diagnostic Reading Test, Pupil Progress Series-Advanced	7–8	Reading for meaning; recall; locating info., etc.	2	65	Anderhalter, Gawkowski & Colstock; Scholastic Testing Service
Durrell Listening-Reading Series Advanced (1969)	7–9	Vocab. listening; reading; paragraph listening, reading	1	80	Durrell; Harcourt, Brace & World
Emporia Reading Tests Jr. High (1964)	7–8	Paragraph reading; word meaning	4	55	Carline, Seybold, Eaton & Sanders; Bureau of Ed'l Measurements

Test	Grade	Measures		Min.	Author; Publisher
Evaluation Aptitude Test (R1952)	12–16+	Neutral Syllogisms, emotionally toned syllogisms; emotional bias; indecision	1	55	Sell; Psychometric Affiliates
Functional Readiness Questionnaire for School & College Students (1957)	1–16	Physical readiness; emotional readiness	1	5	Taylor & Sloan; Reading Study Skills Center
Gates-MacGinitie Reading Tests Survey E (R1965)	7–9	Speed & accuracy; vocabulary; comprehension	6	49	Gates & MacGinitie; Teachers College Press, Columbia University
Gray Oral Reading Test (R1967)	1–16+		4		Gray; Bobbs-Merrill
Individual Placement Series-Reading Adequacy "READ" Test (R1966)	12+	Reading rate; per cent of comprehension; corrected reading rate	1	10–15	Norman; Personnel Research Associates
Iowa Silent Reading Tests Advanced (R1942)	9–14	Rate; comprehension; etc.	4	60	Green, Jorgensen, Kelley; Harcourt, Brace & World
Iowa Tests of Educational Development: Test 5: Ability to Interpret Reading Materials in Social Studies (R1961)	9–12		2	70	Science Research Associates
Test 6: Ability ... Natural Sciences (R1961)	9–12		2	70	Science Research Associates
Test 9: Use of	9–12		2	35	Science Research Associates
Kelley-Greene Reading Comprehension Test (1952)	9–13	Paragraph Comprehension; directed reading; retention of details, reading rate	1	75	Kelley & Greene; Harcourt, Brace & World

135

Test	Grade	Content	No.	Min.	Publisher
Library Survey Test Test 1 (1967)	7–8	General info; misc. info.	1		Perfection Form Co.
Library Sources & Skills Test II (1967) Test III (1967)	9–10 11–12	Library references Library references	1 1		Perfection Form Co. Perfection Form Co.
Logical Reasoning (1955)	9–16+		1	25	Hertzka & Guilford; Sheridan Psychological Svc.
Maintaining Reading Efficiency Tests (1966)	9–16	Rate comprehension accuracy; reading efficiency	2		Peeples & Taylor; Developmental Reading Distributors
Metropolitan Achievement Tests Advanced (R1962)	7–9	Word knowledge; reading	3	46	Durost, Bixler, Hildreth, Lund & Wrightstone; Harcourt, Brace & World
Minn. Reading Exam for College Students (R1935)	9–16	Vocabulary; paragraph reading	2	55	Haggerty & Eurich; Univ. of Minnesota Press
Minn. Speed of Reading Test for College Students (R1936)	12–16	History; geography; economics, government; psychology; education; science	2	15	Eurich; University of Minnesota Press
Nat'l Achievement Tests: High School Test (R1952)	7–12	Vocabulary; word discrimination, details, etc.	2	40	Speer & Smith; Acorn Pub. Co., Psychometric Affiliates
Nelson-Denny Reading Test: Vocab-Comp. Rate (R1960)	9–16+	Vocabulary; comprehension; rate	2	35	Nelson, Denny, Brown; Houghton Mifflin

Test	Grade	Description	No.	Time	Author; Publisher
Peabody Info. Test					
High School (1940)	9–12	Library exam	1	35	Shores & Moore; Educational Test Bureau
College (R1940)	13–16		1	37	
Pictographic Self Rating Scale (R1957)	9–16		1	35	Ryden; Acorn Pub. Co., Psychometric Affiliates
Purdue Reading Test for Ind'l Supervisors (1955)	12+		1	35	Tiffin & Dunlap; Purdue Research Foundation
Purdue Reading Test (R1953)	7–16		2	45	Remmers, Stalnaker & Baker; State High School Testing Service for Ind.
RBH Reading Comprehension Test (R1963)	12+		1	25	Richardson, Bellows, Henry & Company
RBH Scientific Reading Test (R1962)	12+		1		Richardson, Bellows, Henry & Company
Reader's Inventory (1963)	9–16+		1		Spache & Taylor; Ed'l Developmental Lab.
Reader Rater with Self Scoring Profile (R1965)	10–12+	Speed; comprehension; reading habits, etc.	1	60–120	Better Reading Program
Reading Eye (R1960)	1–16+	Fixations; Regressions, comprehension; efficiency	8	4	Taylor & Frackenpohl, Educational Developmental Laboratories
Reading for Understanding Placement Test-Sr. (R1965)	8–12		1		Thurstone; Science Res. Associates

Test	Grade	Description	No.	Time	Author / Publisher
Reading Versatility Test		Rate of reading; comprehension: skimming; scanning			McDonald, Alodia & Nason; Ed'l Dev. Laboratories
Intermediate (R1962)	8–12		1		Zimmy & Byrne, Ed. Dev. Laboratories
Advanced (R1962)	12–16		4	30	
Robinson-Hall Reading Tests (R1949)	13–16	Reading ability for art, history, fiction; rate, comprehension	5		Robinson & Hall; Univ. Pub. Sales, Ohio State University
Scholastic Tests-Ed-Dev. Series Senior (1965)	9–12		2	360	Anderhalter, etc.. Scholastic Testing Svc.
Scharmmel-Gray H.S. & College Test (R1942)	7–16	Gross-comp.; comp.-efficiency; rate	2	30	Schrammel & Gray; Bobbs-Merrill
Sequential Tests of Educational Progress-Reading		Ability to recall, translate, make inferences; ability to analyze motivation, presentation; ability to criticize			Cooperative Test. Div., Educational Testing Service
Level 1 (R1963)	13–14		2	90–100	
Level 2 (R1963)	10–12		2	90–100	
Level 3 (R1963)	7–9		2	90–100	
SRA Reading Progress Test (R1963)	12+	Vocabulary; logical thinking; reading for information; rate	1		Science Research Assoc.
SRA Tests of Ed'l Ability		Language; reasoning; quantitative			
Level II (R1962)	6–9		1	67	Thurstone, SRA
Level III (R1962)	9–12		1	45	Thurstone, SRA
SRA Youth Inventory (R1960)	9–12	School, future, self, health, things in general	1	30–45	Remmers, Drucher & Shimberg SRA
Standard Achievement Tests- Adv. Paragraph Meaning (R1966)	7–9	Paragraph meaning	1	35	Kelley, Madden, Gardner & Rudman; Harcourt, Brace & World

Test	Grades	Forms	Time (min.)	Content	Publisher
Study Habits Checklist (R1967)	9–16	1			Preston & Botel; SRA
Study Habits Inventory (R1941)	12–16	1	10–20		Wrenn; Consulting Psychologists Press
Study Performance Test (R1943)	9–16	1			Toops & Shover; Wilbur L. Layton Pub.
Study Skills Counseling Eval. (1962)	7–16	1	10–20	Study time, conditions; taking notes; examinations; habits & attitudes	Demos; Western Psychological Services
Survey of Study Habits & Attitudes (R1967)	7–14	2	25–35	Study habits, attitudes	Brown & Holtzman; Psychological Corp.
Survey of Study Habits Experimental Edition (1944)	8–14	1	30		Traxler; Educational Records Bureau
Test on the Use of the Dictionary (R1963)	9–16	1	30–40	Pronunciation; usage spelling; derivation	Spache; Reading Lab. & Clinic, U. of Florida

glossary of terms

auditory reader—A person who imagines or hears words pronounced while reading silently and often creates unnecessary mental pictures of the subject matter being read.

comprehension—The understanding of what is read.

concentration—The focusing of the mind on what is read.

eye span—The amount of type seen in one stop of the eyes.

fixation—The stopping of the eyes to focus upon a word or groups of words.

flexible reading; flexibility—Adaptation of reading rate to purpose. Speeding up the reading rate on easy or familiar reading; slowing down on difficult reading.

grouping—The training of the eyes to read more words per fixation and to read these groups more quickly, thereby reducing fixations per line and the time per fixation.

indentation—Reading with the first fixation of the eyes on each line, and the last fixation on each line, indented several letters from the margins.

motor reader—A reader who uses his motor skills (tongue, lips, larynx) to form the words as he reads silently.

mumbleread—To repeat a nonsense word or two while reading aloud in order to overcome vocalizing.

pacer—An object used on a page of print to pull the eyes along the line of print at a faster rate.

pacing—Focusing the eyes to move in directed patterns across the line and down the page.

previewing—Quickly passing over the reading material in order to acquaint the reader with the subject matter before beginning actual reading.

rapid reading instruction—Training which enables one to increase reading efficiency through conscientious application of developmental reading principles.

rapid return—Pulling the pacing hand back to the beginning of the next line to be read as rapidly as possible.

reaming—Reading with unconsciously fluctuating speeds varying from slow reading speeds to skimming speeds, even within one paragraph.

regression—An involuntary movement of the eyes back over material already covered.

retention—The capacity for remembering reading information over a period of time.

scanning—Briefly fixating on the beginning of a paragraph first, then on the middle and end, to locate specific facts.

skimming—Reading the first sentence (topic sentence) of each paragraph and then rapidly passing the eyes over the rest of the paragraph, looking for main ideas.

visual reader—One who passes the words directly from the page to his comprehension without any unnecessary vocalizing or subvocalizing.

vocabulary—The words an individual understands and uses in reading, listening, speaking or writing.

vocalizing—Sounding words aloud or silently with the tongue, lips or in the larynx while reading silently.

index